British
BIRDS

Written by
Duncan Brewer

Illustrated by
Alan Harris, Ian Jackson

Miles Kelly

Contents

GARDEN AND COUNTRYSIDE BIRDS 10—123

SEA AND COASTAL BIRDS 124—213

How to use this book

Each bird profile has a paragraph of text, an illustration and essential statistics. Useful checklists help with identification and you can add your own notes and drawings. Photos and captions provide extra information.

Pictures of birds in their natural habitats.

Questions to help you successfully identify birds.

Did it have a red face and breast? ◯

Did it have a high-pitched, sweet song? ◯

Was the rest of the bird light brown? ◯

Was its belly white? ◯

Young, or juvenile, robins lack the characteristic colour of their parents. The dull plumage allows them to hide from predators.

My observations

Make notes about what you have seen or heard.

Try sketching the birds you see, or make a photo album by adding photographs you have taken.

my drawings and photos

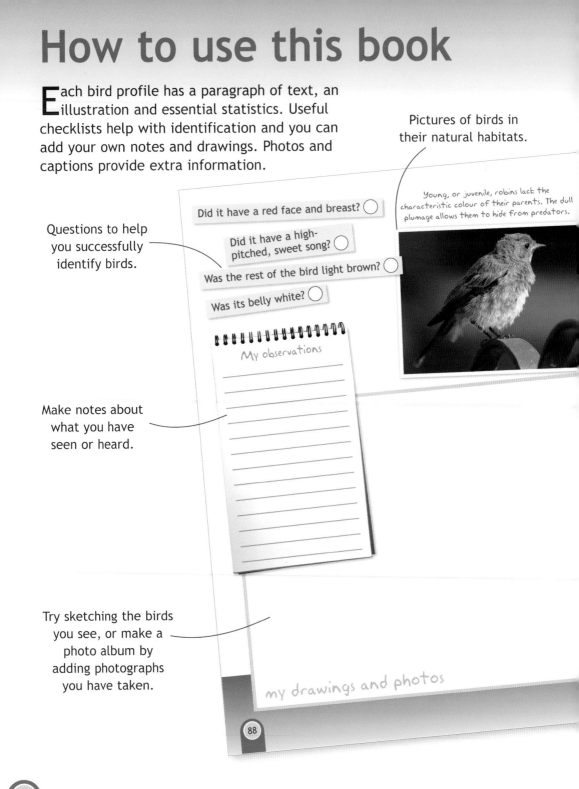

Each bird's name is given, together with its scientific name.

This tab helps you to identify bird families — use the contents on pages 4 and 5.

Robin
(Erithacus rubecula)

Probably Britain's most easily recognised bird, the robin is perfectly at home in the garden. It is famous for boldly coming close to anyone digging, in the hope of catching worms and grubs that are dug up. The robin sings to establish its territorial boundaries, and attract mates. It defends its territory with extreme aggression, and has even been known to fight to the death. In very harsh weather robins may observe a temporary truce, and you could see several feeding together at the bird table. Unafraid of humans, they rapidly become almost hand-tame when provided with regular food.

Read the main paragraph to get key information about each bird.

SIZE
Length 14 cm, Weight 16–22 g

COLOUR
MALE Light brown crown, back, tail and wings. Face and breast bright orange-red. Undersides white with buff tinge, with bands of white extending round the red breast, up and over the eyes.
FEMALE Same as male.
WINTER DIFFERENCES None.

NEST
Domed, made of grass, wool, moss, hair. In hole in bank or wall. Sometimes in sheds, in old buckets and other containers.

CALL
'Tik-tik'. Sweet, high-pitched twittery song.

RESIDENT/VISITOR
Resident. Joined by paler-coloured visitors from northern Europe in winter.

A factfile of information and special features about each bird.

brown plumage on back and wings

red face and breast

white feathers underneath

♂ ♀

QUICK ID
• Upright shape and red breast
• Great territorial aggression, especially in spring
• Bold approach to humans
• Fluffed out almost spherical in cold weather

Useful points for identifying different species.

BEST TIME TO SPOT

6
5
4
3
2
1
0
JAN FEB MAR APR MAY JUN JUL AUG SEP OCT NOV DEC

89

When is the best time of year to spot a bird?
1 = unlikely 6 = very likely

Sometimes both sexes of the same species have different plumage or bills. Use the male and female symbols to help you identify different sexes.

♂ Male   ♀ Female

How to birdwatch

Birdwatching is a rewarding and healthy activity. You learn not just about birds but about all aspects of the natural world, including other animals, plants, weather, the seasons and the landscape.

All you need to start birdwatching is a notebook, a pencil, a bird guide, and the ability to sit still for a few minutes at a time. Large amounts of expensive weatherproof clothing are not essential. However, if you intend to watch birds at the coast, or elsewhere in the open, it is a good idea to have sensible footwear and a waterproof jacket. Wear enough layers to keep warm, and take a flask of hot drink and some food.

Using binoculars will help you study birds in great detail.

A pair of binoculars is likely to be your most expensive item of equipment. You can birdwatch without binoculars, but with them you can see small details that you would otherwise miss, and get a really close look at birds without scaring them. Binoculars usually have numbers on them, such as 8x30, or 9x40. The numbers give information about how big and how bright the binoculars make things look. A good size for general birdwatching is 8x30.

Be prepared and pack a map and compass. Take a hot drink and food too.

Bird feeders are a great way to encourage birds into your garden.

Remember to leave details of your intended destination for someone back at base.

Take notes of what you see. These will help you identify your sightings later, with the aid of your handbook. A waterproof map case will keep your notes dry despite rain and spray.

Blend in. Wear subdued colours and avoid making sudden movements and sounds. Birds are particularly wary when feeding.

Keep a record of your sightings, along with sketches and photographs, for future reference.

The garden is an ideal place to watch birdlife. A bird table, bird feeder or nesting box will encourage a huge variety of species. Hedges and trees are homes and hunting grounds to a number of birds. Sitting by a window birdwatching can be rewarding whatever the time of day.

If you have chosen a site to watch sea or coastal birds, it is a good idea to have an Ordnance Survey map of the area. This will help you find other likely sites within walking distance.

On the coast many birdwatching sites include cliffs and rocky bays. Never attempt to climb cliffs to get closer to birds. Most cliffs are extremely dangerous due to loose rock, and seabirds are quite likely to attack anyone getting anywhere near their nests. You should never disturb a nest or take an egg. If you are down at sea level to watch birds, make sure you know what time the tide comes in and leave plenty of time to get clear.

Always put your safety first at cliffs and by the coast.

How to identify birds

A good way to start learning how to identify birds is to pick one bird and study it for as long as it remains in view, and listen to its call.

Have a small notebook and pen nearby and write down bird names, and the date and time of day. Give birds you do not recognize a number and a page to themselves. Jot down a few notes about each one. How big is it — sparrow-sized? Smaller? Blackbird-sized? Larger? What is its main colour? What other colours and markings does it have? Black cap? Speckled breast? Note the bird's main body colour, and also variations such as differently coloured head or wings. What colour are its beak and legs? What shape is its tail? Are its legs long or short?

As well as writing notes, try to sketch what you see. You can always add your sketches to the notes area in this handbook.

When you have noted as much as you can about its appearance, try to describe its calls. Add notes about how it flies, how it behaves if it is feeding, and what you think it is eating.

If you get the chance, take some photos. It's a great way to study adult birds and their young.

Your sketches don't need to be overly detailed, and they are a good way of showing which birds come to the bird table.

Now briefly describe the habitat. In the garden, is it the bird table or the hedge where birds come to feed and forage? When identifying nesting sea and coastal birds you will have to learn which birds nest on cliff ledges or on shingle, which in burrows or on marshland.

Once you have described your bird to the best of your ability, it is time to check your handbook. Can you recognize your bird from its picture and description?

From now on, try to use the same terms as the handbook for parts of a bird's body. Use 'cap' for the top of the head, 'nape' for the back of the

neck and so on. The more you learn and use the correct terms, the better you can describe what you see.

One problem, especially with seabirds, is that the young often have very different plumage from their parents despite being the same size. Often the young of different species look very similar. Watching which adults feed a young bird should help identification.

When writing notes use headings such as colour, markings, habitat, shape, size, flight, call. Also record the date, as birds often spend the seasons in different places.

The more you watch, the more you will see, and your identification will become more accurate.

Before long you will be familiar with several species, and each birdwatching session will add knowledge and make you more confident in your fascinating new hobby.

After a day of birdwatching, add your notes and pictures to your handbook.

GARDEN AND COUNTRYSIDE BIRDS

Did its feathers look glossy? ◯

Was its bill yellow? ◯

Did it walk in a jerky way? ◯

Was it noisy or aggressive? ◯

With their metallic colours, adult starlings are easy to recognise. Juveniles, however, have plain brown feathers and a dark bill.

My observations

my drawings and photos

Starling

(Sturnus vulgaris)

The starling is one of the commonest birds to be seen in the British Isles, although its numbers are currently in decline. Starlings are noisy and energetic, and a small flock can clear a bird table of food in a matter of seconds. Winter flocks flying to roost may number thousands of birds, swooping and wheeling in unison, and chattering noisily once roosted. Enthusiastic birdbath visitors, starlings dip and shake vigorously, then preen, spreading oil from a rump gland over all their feathers before smoothing them back into shape.

SIZE

Length 22 cm, Weight 75–90 g

COLOUR

MALE Metallic sheen to most feathers, with pale feather tips. Light-brown edging to wing feathers.
FEMALE Similar to male.
WINTER DIFFERENCES Bill turns dark. Feather tips brighter after autumn moult, giving a speckled appearance.

NEST

Untidy straw, grass and feathers. Usually in a hole in trees, buildings, cliffs, nest boxes.

CALL

Harsh 'tcheer'. Song – whistles, clicks and mimicry of other birds and other sounds.

RESIDENT/VISITOR

Resident, with some winter visitors from northern Europe.

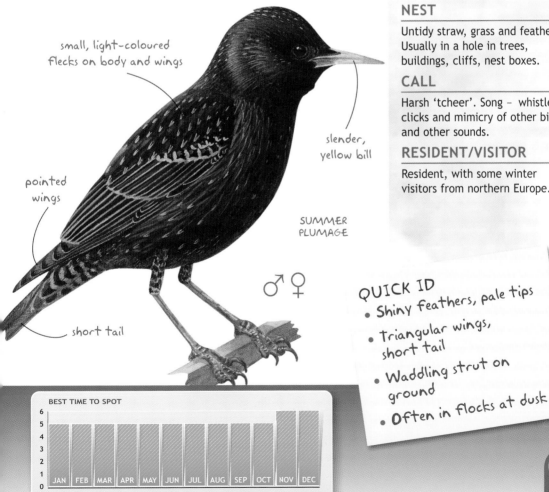

small, light-coloured flecks on body and wings

pointed wings

slender, yellow bill

short tail

SUMMER PLUMAGE

♂ ♀

QUICK ID
- Shiny feathers, pale tips
- Triangular wings, short tail
- Waddling strut on ground
- Often in flocks at dusk

BEST TIME TO SPOT

	JAN	FEB	MAR	APR	MAY	JUN	JUL	AUG	SEP	OCT	NOV	DEC

Did it repeat its song phrase three or four times? ○

Did it run and hop? ○

Did you see evidence of smashed snail shells? ○

Did it have a spotted breast? ○

A female song thrush lays between three and five eggs in each brood. She can produce two or three broods in the spring/summer.

My observations

my drawings and photos

Song thrush
(Turdus philomelos)

The song thrush is the most familiar of the garden 'spotted' thrushes. It can be seen, sometimes in pairs, moving in runs and hops as it hunts worms, snails and insects. Once more common than the blackbird, its numbers have fallen in recent years. A sure sign of a song thrush is a stone 'anvil', surrounded by the broken shells of snails it has hammered open. The song thrush also eats soft fruit and berries, and is particularly fond of yew berries. It is more likely to appear in garden shrubbery than at the bird table.

SIZE
Length 23 cm, Weight 70–90 g

COLOUR
MALE Brown back, buff underparts. Spotted breast.
FEMALE Same as male.
WINTER DIFFERENCES None.

NEST
Dried stems lined with mud and rotting wood, bound with saliva that dries hard. Trees, hedges, shed rafters.

CALL
Loud 'tchuk'. In flight – 'sip'. Song – flute-like repeated phrases.

RESIDENT/VISITOR
Mainly resident, though some migrate south.

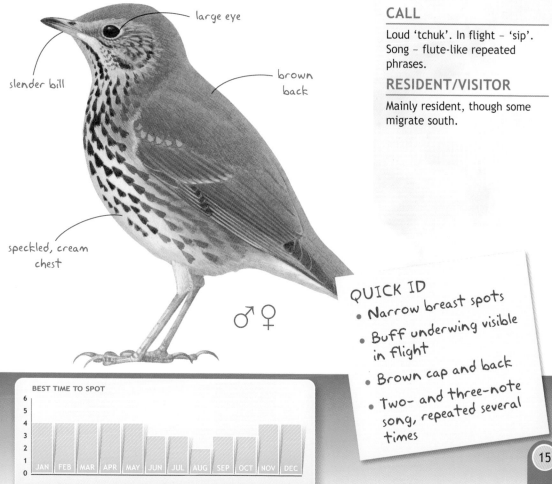

large eye

slender bill

brown back

speckled, cream chest

♂ ♀

QUICK ID
- Narrow breast spots
- Buff underwing visible in flight
- Brown cap and back
- Two- and three-note song, repeated several times

BEST TIME TO SPOT

| JAN | FEB | MAR | APR | MAY | JUN | JUL | AUG | SEP | OCT | NOV | DEC |

Was it larger than a song thrush? ◯

Was it perched at the top of a tree? ◯

Did it have white patches under its wings? ◯

Did it have a spotted breast? ◯

My observations

In the winter, male mistle thrushes often defend trees where they have found plenty of juicy berries, scaring other birds away.

my drawings and photos

Mistle thrush
(Turdus viscivorus)

The mistle thrush is the largest British thrush. It is also known as the 'storm cock', because it sings from the treetops when winds are blowing hard. It forages on the ground for insects, worms and snails in spring and summer. It feeds on fruit and berries in winter, including yew, hawthorn, holly, mistletoe and ivy. Although usually nervous of humans, and uncommon at the bird table, the mistle thrush can be very aggressive in the breeding season, even attacking dogs and gardeners. You can see it in most terrains, from gardens and orchards to woodland, moorland and other wild country.

SIZE
Length 27 cm, Weight 110–140 g

COLOUR
MALE Grey-brown back, buff underparts, pure white underwing. Dark spots on breast.
FEMALE Similar to male.
WINTER DIFFERENCES None.

NEST
Grass and moss, reinforced with earth, with moss, grass and feathers around rim. Situated in fork of tree.

CALL
Harsh 'churr' during flight.

RESIDENT/VISITOR
Mainly resident. Some winter in Europe, while others migrate to the British Isles from northern Europe in autumn.

grey-brown back

sturdy bill

long wings

whitish breast with dark spots

powerful, long legs

♂ ♀

QUICK ID
- Large size compared to other thrushes
- Grey upperparts
- Dark, broad spots on breast
- White underwing visible in flight

BEST TIME TO SPOT

6 5 4 3 2 1 0

JAN FEB MAR APR MAY JUN JUL AUG SEP OCT NOV DEC

Did it have a bold eyebrow marking? ◯

Was its bill short and thin? ◯

Were its flanks chestnut red in colour? ◯

Was it smaller than other thrushes? ◯

Redwings can survive very cold weather. They ruffle up their feathers to improve the insulation that their plumage provides.

My observations

_____
_____
_____
_____
_____
_____
_____
_____
_____
_____
_____
_____
_____

my drawings and photos

Redwing

(Turdus iliacus)

Unlike the garden thrushes, the redwing is most commonly found in woods and fields in flocks, foraging for worms, slugs, snails, insects and berries. Sometimes it mixes with fieldfares and song thrushes. A flock of redwings will congregate on a berry tree and strip it bare before moving on. It breeds in open spruce and birch woods in northern Europe. It visits Britain in winter, and when freezing weather makes life difficult, it may visit the garden to feed from the bird table, or forage through flower borders. Flocks of migrating redwings can be identified at night by their piping calls.

SIZE
Length 21 cm, Weight 55–75 g

COLOUR
MALE Olive-brown back and pale underparts. Chestnut flanks and underwing. White eye stripe. Spotted breast.
FEMALE Similar to male.
WINTER DIFFERENCES None.

NEST
Dry grass, moss and mud. Usually in trees and bushes, sometimes on the ground.

CALL
'Seeip' in flight.

RESIDENT/VISITOR
A winter visitor from northern Europe, Siberia and Iceland. Some pairs have bred in northern Scotland.

bold white eye stripe

♂ ♀

silver-white feathers on underside with speckles

chestnut-red flanks

QUICK ID
- Moves and feeds in flocks
- Creamy white eye stripe
- Chestnut underwing visible in flight
- Smaller than other thrushes

BEST TIME TO SPOT

	JAN	FEB	MAR	APR	MAY	JUN	JUL	AUG	SEP	OCT	NOV	DEC

Was its back chestnut brown? ◯

Was its tail black? ◯

Did it have a distinctive blue-grey head? ◯

Was it in a flock? ◯

My observations

_____
_____
_____
_____
_____
_____
_____
_____
_____
_____
_____
_____
_____

Fieldfares strip trees of their berries in winter, and are often joined by other birds such as redwings, blackbirds and mistle thrushes.

my drawings and photos

Fieldfare

(Turdus pilaris)

This large and colourful thrush forages in noisy, chattering flocks in open fields and parks. As it feeds, the flock moves steadily forwards across the ground. In cold winter weather it eagerly joins other birds at the bird table. It also visits orchards to feed on rotten fruit still lying on the ground. Interestingly, whether feeding on the ground or roosting in a tree, the entire flock faces the same way. Fieldfares take off and wheel in flight all in unison, constantly calling. They usually roost together on the ground, among shrubs and bushes, and even in the furrows of ploughed fields.

SIZE
Length 26 cm, Weight 80–130 g

COLOUR
MALE Blue-grey head and rump. Rusty brown back. Throat and breast, buff-yellow, with dark spots. White underbelly and underwings. Black tail.
FEMALE Similar to male.
WINTER DIFFERENCES None.

NEST
Untidy straw, grass, feathers. Usually in a hole in trees, buildings, cliffs, nest boxes.

CALL
'Ee-eep' on ground. 'Chack-chack-chack' in flight.

RESIDENT/VISITOR
A winter visitor from Scandinavia and northern Europe.

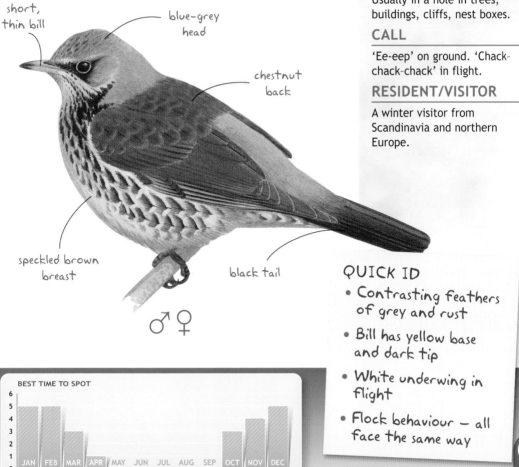

short, thin bill

blue-grey head

chestnut back

speckled brown breast

black tail

♂ ♀

QUICK ID
- Contrasting feathers of grey and rust
- Bill has yellow base and dark tip
- White underwing in flight
- Flock behaviour — all face the same way

BEST TIME TO SPOT

| JAN | FEB | MAR | APR | MAY | JUN | JUL | AUG | SEP | OCT | NOV | DEC |

Was its bill bright orange-yellow? ○

Were its feathers pure black? ○

Was its song melodious? ○

Was it feeding on the ground? ○

My observations

_____
_____
_____
_____
_____
_____
_____
_____
_____
_____
_____
_____
_____

Young blackbirds can be mistaken for thrushes. They have pale streaks on their backs, reddish-brown mottled breasts and dark bills.

my drawings and photos

Blackbird
(Turdus merula)

The blackbird is a member of the thrush family. It is one of the most common garden birds and is found throughout Europe. Hopping and running along the ground, it scuffles noisily through dead leaves for worms, insects, fallen fruits and seeds. It is often seen tugging earthworms out of garden lawns, but stays close to leafy cover. The blackbird is an enthusiastic visitor to the bird table. It is one of the earliest members of the dawn chorus, and likes to sit high on a tree or roof-top to sing its melodious, fluting song.

SIZE
Length 25 cm, Weight 80–110 g

COLOUR
MALE Coal-black plumage. Bright orange-yellow bill and eye ring.
FEMALE Dark-brown back. Pale undersides. Mottled breast.
WINTER DIFFERENCES None.

NEST
Moss and grass, plastered with mud, lined with soft grass. In trees, hedges, wall ivy.

CALL
'Tchink, tchink' when uneasy or settling for the night. 'Tchook' when anxious. Loud cackling alarm.

RESIDENT/VISITOR
Resident, with some winter visitors from northern Europe.

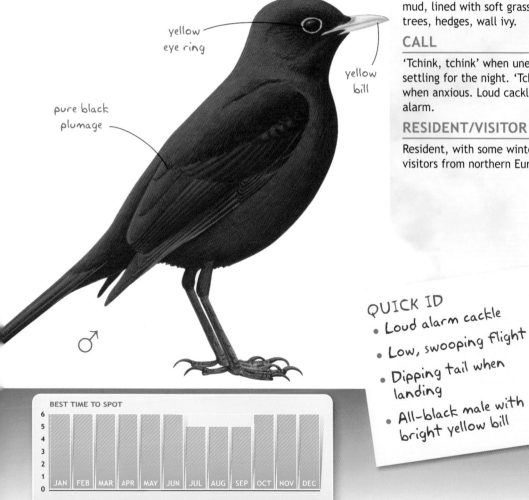

yellow eye ring

yellow bill

pure black plumage

♂

QUICK ID
- Loud alarm cackle
- Low, swooping flight
- Dipping tail when landing
- All-black male with bright yellow bill

BEST TIME TO SPOT

	JAN	FEB	MAR	APR	MAY	JUN	JUL	AUG	SEP	OCT	NOV	DEC

Was its song remarkably melodic? ◯

Was its tail spread in song display? ◯

Was it reddish-brown in colour? ◯

Was it seen in a wooded area? ◯

My observations

_____
_____
_____
_____
_____
_____
_____
_____
_____
_____
_____
_____
_____

Young nightingales practise their songs in preparation for adulthood. Juveniles have spotted backs and speckled breasts.

my drawings and photos

Nightingale
(Luscinia megarhynchos)

The nightingale is famously known for its beautiful, melodic song. It may be heard after dark but also sings during the daytime. It is an unobtrusive reddish-brown bird with a longish, rounded tail that it spreads in song display. The nightingale is not an easy bird to observe as it inhabits areas of dense thicket and scrub vegetation, but the male can often be spotted perching openly to sing. Its numbers are currently in decline. Nightingales are most likely to be seen in the southeast of England.

SIZE
Length 17 cm, Weight 17–24 g

COLOUR
MALE Reddish brown with white throat and creamy breast. Short, brown pointed bill.
FEMALE As male.
WINTER DIFFERENCES None.

NEST
Well-hidden at ground level. A thick cup of dead leaves lined with fine hair and grass.

CALL
Melodious song of trills, 'peeoo' at beginning, harsh 'tchak' and 'whooeet' notes.

RESIDENT/VISITOR
Summer visitor.

red-brown upper feathers

RARE

white throat and cream underbelly

long reddish tail

♂♀

QUICK ID
- Beautiful song of liquid trills that grows in loudness
- Characteristic red tail

BEST TIME TO SPOT

| | | | | | | | | | | | |
|6|
|5|
|4|
|3|
|2|
|1|
|0| JAN | FEB | MAR | APR | MAY | JUN | JUL | AUG | SEP | OCT | NOV | DEC |

Did it have white cheeks? ◯

Was its tail pale blue and notched in shape? ◯

Was its breast yellow with a dark dividing line? ◯

Did it flit about? ◯

My observations

_____
_____
_____
_____
_____
_____
_____
_____
_____
_____
_____
_____

A single brood of blue tits may contain up to 16 chicks. Both the male and female feed the chicks, especially upon caterpillars and seeds.

my drawings and photos

Blue tit

(Cyanistes caeruleus)

One of nature's great acrobats, the blue tit prefers oak and birch trees in the wild, and has become one of the commonest garden birds. Frequently seen at the bird table, it repays its hosts by also feeding on garden pests such as greenfly. It readily hangs upside down to feed on lumps of fat or coconut halves suspended on a string. Sometimes it is known as the tomtit. The blue tit quickly becomes tame around humans.

SIZE

Length 11.5 cm, Weight 11 g

COLOUR

MALE Blue crown, wings and tail. Head white at sides. Black stripe through eye. Yellow underparts. Greenish back.
FEMALE Similar to male.
WINTER DIFFERENCES None.

NEST

Hair, wool or feathers on moss and dried grass. In holes, including trees, walls, banks, and even letterboxes. Readily uses nest boxes.

CALL

'Tsie-tsi-tsi'.

RESIDENT/VISITOR

Resident.

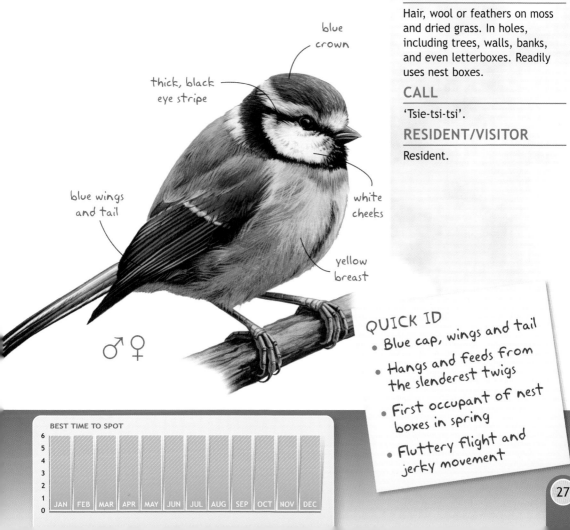

blue crown

thick, black eye stripe

blue wings and tail

white cheeks

yellow breast

♂ ♀

QUICK ID
- Blue cap, wings and tail
- Hangs and feeds from the slenderest twigs
- First occupant of nest boxes in spring
- Fluttery flight and jerky movement

BEST TIME TO SPOT

JAN	FEB	MAR	APR	MAY	JUN	JUL	AUG	SEP	OCT	NOV	DEC

6
5
4
3
2
1
0

Was it small in size? ◯

Did it have two white wing bars? ◯

Was its voice high-pitched? ◯

Did it have a black bib? ◯

Coal tits often hide food, such as insects, spiders, seeds and nuts, amongst the tufts of pine needles, collecting it later.

My observations

_____
_____
_____
_____
_____
_____
_____
_____
_____
_____
_____
_____
_____

my drawings and photos

Coal tit

(Periparus ater)

The coal tit is the smallest member of the tit family and is much shyer than the blue tit. It occasionally uses a nest box, and will visit the bird table, but carries food away and hides it. The coal tit is naturally a bird of the forest. It forages in trees for live prey such as spiders and insects, and searches the ground for nuts and seeds. It has a preference for deep woods of conifers. An acrobatic bird, it can be seen creeping up tree trunks. It sometimes forages with mixed flocks of goldcrests and treecreepers through trees and bracken. The male sings its breeding calls from high in a tall tree.

SIZE

Length 11.5 cm, Weight 9–11 g

COLOUR

MALE Olive-brown back. Buff underparts, paler on breast. White cheeks, with a black cap and throat. White nape. White wing bars.
FEMALE Similar to male.
WINTER DIFFERENCES None.

NEST

In a hole, lined with moss, grass, hair or wool. Low in a tree stump, wall, sometimes on the ground.

CALL

'Tsui' or 'tsee'.

RESIDENT/VISITOR

Resident.

white cheek and nape

small size

black bib

white wing bars

♂ ♀

QUICK ID
- Small and plump with a short tail
- White patch on nape
- Double white wing bars
- Feeds very high in pine trees

BEST TIME TO SPOT

	JAN	FEB	MAR	APR	MAY	JUN	JUL	AUG	SEP	OCT	NOV	DEC

Was it bigger and bolder than other tits? ◯

Did it have white cheeks? ◯

Did it have a yellow bib and chest? ◯

Did it have a breast stripe? ◯

An adult great tit may have to find food for as many as 11 chicks at a time. Both parents feed the chicks, and keep the nest clean.

My observations

_____
_____
_____
_____
_____
_____
_____
_____
_____
_____
_____
_____

my drawings and photos

Great tit

(Parus major)

The energetic great tit is one of the bullies of the bird table, boisterously driving off shyer birds as it muscles in on the free meal. It is the largest of the British tits, but is still extremely acrobatic. It will happily swing upside down to peck at a suet ball on a string. Great tits have powerful beaks, and can be seen holding down nuts and other tough items with a foot to hammer away. They can even open hazelnuts with this technique. Despite appearing regularly in the garden, great tits are woodland birds. In winter they often forage in flocks over woodland floors, scratching for food.

SIZE

Length 14 cm, Weight 19 g

COLOUR

MALE Olive-green back, bright yellow underparts. Black cap circles white cheeks to join black throat, leading to wide black stripe to tail. Blue-grey rump, tail and wings. White wing bar and outer tail feathers.
FEMALE Similar to male.
WINTER DIFFERENCES None.

NEST

Moss, lined with feathers and hair. In holes in trees, walls and hollow fence posts.

CALL

Metallic 'ching'. Loud 'teacher-teacher' song.

RESIDENT/VISITOR

Resident.

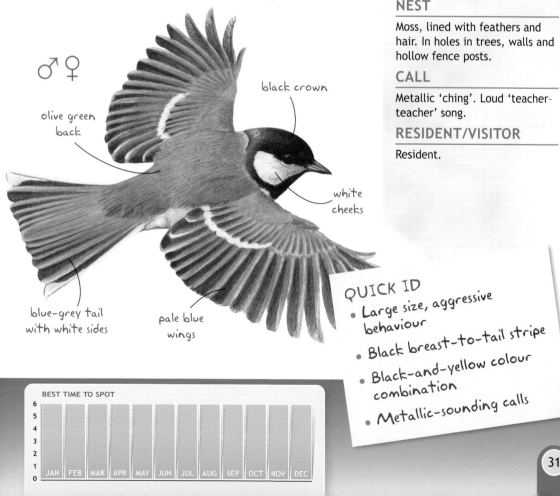

♂ ♀

olive green back

black crown

white cheeks

blue-grey tail with white sides

pale blue wings

QUICK ID
- Large size, aggressive behaviour
- Black breast-to-tail stripe
- Black-and-yellow colour combination
- Metallic-sounding calls

BEST TIME TO SPOT

JAN	FEB	MAR	APR	MAY	JUN	JUL	AUG	SEP	OCT	NOV	DEC

6
5
4
3
2
1
0

Did it have a tail longer than its body? ○

Were its underparts white and pink? ○

Did it have a bold, black stripe over its eyes? ○

Did it have a white crown? ○

My observations

_____
_____
_____
_____
_____
_____
_____
_____
_____
_____
_____
_____

Long-tailed tits have tiny, weak bills that are best suited to collecting small mouthfuls of food that other birds may overlook.

my drawings and photos

Long-tailed tit
(Aegithalos caudatus)

Apart from its long tail, this is one of our tiniest birds. It is not a true member of the tit family, and usually moves in small flocks seeking insects for food. Because of its small size, it is vulnerable to cold, and flock members huddle together to keep warm at night. Parents also cram themselves into the nest with up to a dozen young. The long-tailed tit was almost exterminated by severe frosts in 1947 in Britain. It uses its tiny beak to harvest insects, and also feeds on buds, and small amounts of lichen and algae in the trees.

SIZE
Length 14 cm, Weight 8 g

COLOUR
MALE Dull white throat and head, with black stripes over the eye, leading to black on upper neck and back. Rosy shoulder patches, lower back and underparts. Black wings and tail. Partly white outer tail feathers.
FEMALE Same as male.
WINTER DIFFERENCES None.

NEST
An oval of moss, wool, spiders' webs and lichen, lined with of feathers. Side entry hole. Built in thick hedges, holly bushes, ivy-clad trees.

CALL
'Zee-zee' and 'trrr'.

RESIDENT/VISITOR
Resident.

bold eyebrow markings

pink shoulder patches

long tail

fluffy pink-and-white plumage

small, round body

♂ ♀

QUICK ID
- Long tail, small, round body
- Fluffy pink-and-white plumage
- Communal huddling at night
- Broad black line over eye

BEST TIME TO SPOT

6											
5											
4											
3											
2											
1											
0	JAN	FEB	MAR	APR	MAY	JUN	JUL	AUG	SEP	OCT	NOV	DEC

Did it have a short, stubby bill? ○

Was its cap glossy black? ○

Was it an elegant-looking little bird? ○

Was its flight flitting and wavy? ○

Marsh tits have whiter breasts than their close cousins, willow tits. They mostly feed on the ground, searching for food in the undergrowth.

My observations

_____
_____
_____
_____
_____
_____
_____
_____
_____
_____
_____
_____

my drawings and photos

Marsh tit

(Poecile palustris)

The marsh tit has been misnamed, for it does not frequent marshes. It prefers woodlands, where it hunts through the trees for insects, and forages on the ground for seeds. It holds tough seeds, such as beechmast, with one foot while it pecks them open with its strong beak. The marsh tit often teams up with roving flocks of other tit species, and it appears in gardens in winter if food is put out. It does not linger at the bird table, but carries food away to eat later, and hides it either in the ground, or in cracks in tree bark.

SIZE
Length 11.5 cm, Weight 11 g

COLOUR
MALE Glossy black cap extending down nape, and a neat black chin patch. Grey-white cheeks, neck sides and underparts. Grey-brown back.
FEMALE Same as male.
WINTER DIFFERENCES None.

NEST
Pad of hair and moss inside a natural hole in a tree, sometimes in a wall. Very rarely in a nest box.

CALL
Shrill 'pitchu'. Song – 'chip, chip, chip'.

RESIDENT/VISITOR
Resident.

short bill

glossy black cap

small, black bib

♂♀

QUICK ID
- Glossy black cap
- Regular ground feeder (unlike the very similar willow tit)
- Distinctive sneeze-like 'pitchu' call
- Smaller head than willow tit

BEST TIME TO SPOT

	JAN	FEB	MAR	APR	MAY	JUN	JUL	AUG	SEP	OCT	NOV	DEC

Was it tiny? ◯

Was its face plain with moustache streak? ◯

Was its body round? ◯

Did it have a distinctive head crest? ◯

The goldcrest is one of Britain's smallest birds. Both adults have a gold crest, but it appears more yellow in females and slightly orange in males.

My observations

_____
_____
_____
_____
_____
_____
_____
_____
_____
_____
_____
_____
_____
_____

my drawings and photos

Goldcrest

(Regulus regulus)

Europe's smallest bird, the goldcrest still manages to migrate across the North Sea from Scandinavia to spend the winter in Britain. Like other tiny birds, it is very vulnerable to severe weather, but always seems to bounce back after cold seasons that almost wipe it out. True to its name, the male goldcrest raises his bright crest when courting, and also when rivals stray into his territory. Goldcrests mingle with tits and firecrests, which are closely related, in food-hunting winter flocks. Their main food consists of spiders and small insects such as aphids. Goldcrests are found in woodland, and in parks and gardens containing conifers such as larch and fir.

SIZE

Length 9 cm, Weight 5–7 g

COLOUR

MALE Dull green back, creamy buff underparts. White bar and black patch on wing. Bright orange crest with black surround.
FEMALE Similar to male, but with paler, lemony crest.
WINTER DIFFERENCES None.

NEST

Basket-shaped nest woven from lichens, moss and spiders' webs, suspended from conifer branches.

CALL

High-pitched 'zeek' and trill. Also 'si-si-si'.

RESIDENT/VISITOR

A partial migrant. Some resident all year round. Others visit for the winter from Scandinavia.

distinctive golden-orange crest

fine moustache streak

♂

round body

QUICK ID
- tiny in size, raisable crest
- Large black eye
- Can hover while hunting insects
- thin, high voice

BEST TIME TO SPOT

	JAN	FEB	MAR	APR	MAY	JUN	JUL	AUG	SEP	OCT	NOV	DEC

Did it have a white eyebrow? ◯

Was its bill long and curved? ◯

Was it well camouflaged? ◯

Was its tail pointed? ◯

My observations

_____
_____
_____
_____
_____
_____
_____
_____
_____
_____
_____
_____
_____

When a treecreeper scales a tree its mottled plumage provides excellent camouflage against the bark, making it hard to spot.

my drawings and photos

Treecreeper

(Certhia familiaris)

The treecreeper is a well camouflaged little bird, but is easily recognised by its long, curving bill, which it uses to probe bark as it creeps up the tree trunk. Almost always working upwards from the bottom of the trunk, the treecreeper uses its stiff tail feathers as a support against the bark. As it creeps upwards it spirals around the tree trunk, then flies down to the bottom of the next tree. The treecreeper occasionally comes into gardens, but will not usually approach the bird table. It can be fed in the garden by smearing fat onto a tree trunk.

SIZE

Length 12.4 cm, Weight 9 g

COLOUR

MALE Brown back with buff streaks. White underparts. White stripe over eye.
FEMALE Similar to male.
WINTER DIFFERENCES None.

NEST

Twigs, grass, moss. Wool and feather lining. In cracks in tree trunks, behind loose bark or ivy, crevices in masonry.

CALL

High-pitched 'tsit'or 'tsee'.

RESIDENT/VISITOR

Resident.

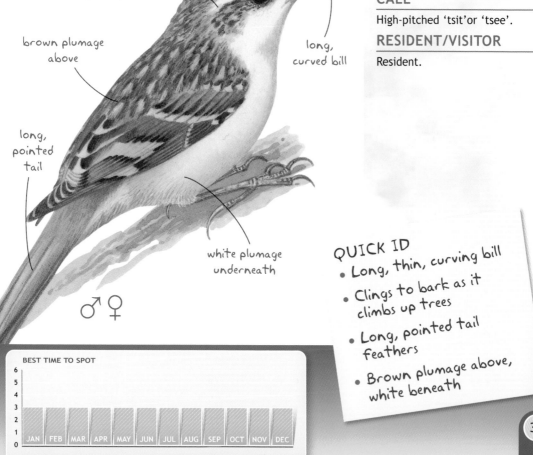

white stripe above eye

brown plumage above

long, curved bill

long, pointed tail

white plumage underneath

♂ ♀

QUICK ID
- Long, thin, curving bill
- Clings to bark as it climbs up trees
- Long, pointed tail feathers
- Brown plumage above, white beneath

BEST TIME TO SPOT

	JAN	FEB	MAR	APR	MAY	JUN	JUL	AUG	SEP	OCT	NOV	DEC
6												
5												
4												
3												
2												
1												
0												

Did it have a bright orange breast? ◯

Was it similar to a chaffinch? ◯

Were its legs red? ◯

Was its belly white? ◯

Although bramblings have been seen in huge flocks numbering thousands in central Europe, smaller flocks are more common in Britain.

My observations

_____

_____

_____

_____

_____

_____

_____

_____

_____

_____

_____

_____

_____

my drawings and photos

Brambling

(Fringilla montifringilla)

The brambling is related to the chaffinch. It is very fond of beech woods, foraging through them in flocks sometimes numbering thousands. When they have eaten all the available food in one place, the flock decamps to find a new supply. When beech-mast crops fail, or when the weather is particularly harsh, the brambling is attracted to gardens where food has been put out. It is basically a ground feeder, and usually takes the seeds and scraps dropped from the table by other birds. Bramblings often move in mixed flocks containing chaffinches and other finches as they hunt for insects and seeds on the woodland floor.

SIZE
Length 14.5 cm, Weight 25 g

COLOUR
MALE Orange breast and shoulders. Black head and back in summer. White rump, with white bands on wings. Red legs.
FEMALE Duller, with brown head and back, and yellowish breast and shoulders.
WINTER DIFFERENCES Male orange-and-black feathers duller due to tips turning brown.

NEST
Moss, plant stalks and lichen. In trees, including conifers.

CALL
'Kvek' when flying. Single 'dzwee' song.

RESIDENT/VISITOR
Winter visitor arriving from Scandinavia in autumn, returning in spring.

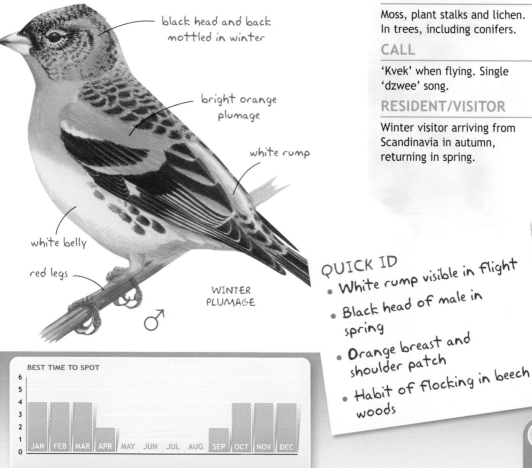

black head and back mottled in winter

bright orange plumage

white rump

white belly

red legs

WINTER PLUMAGE

♂

QUICK ID
- White rump visible in flight
- Black head of male in spring
- Orange breast and shoulder patch
- Habit of flocking in beech woods

BEST TIME TO SPOT

	JAN	FEB	MAR	APR	MAY	JUN	JUL	AUG	SEP	OCT	NOV	DEC

Was its bill thick and stubby? ◯

Did it have a rosy pink breast? ◯

Was its face and crown black? ◯

Was it a thickset bird? ◯

Male and female bullfinches pair for life. They can produce up to three broods in a single breeding season.

My observations

my drawings and photos

Bullfinch
(Pyrrhula pyrrhula)

Bullfinches are often seen in couples, and are thought to pair for life. They are shy, secretive birds, and like to stay close to cover. The bullfinch rarely forages on the ground, and is usually spotted in trees and bushes, using its strong beak to harvest seeds, berries and buds. Its fondness for buds when other food is scarce has made it a very unpopular bird with fruit farmers, as a pair of hungry bullfinches can do severe damage to the growing points of a fruit tree in the spring. In autumn and early winter the bullfinch feeds on seeds such as ash keys. Rare at the bird table, it will take shelled peanuts from a net.

SIZE
Length 15 cm, Weight 21–27 g

COLOUR
MALE Smoke-grey back and rosy red underparts. Black forehead, crown, chin and bill. Black on wings and tail. White wing bars and under base of tail.
FEMALE Pale brown back and pinkish underparts. Hind neck is grey. Black and white as male.
WINTER DIFFERENCES None.

NEST
Twig foundation lined with rootlets and hair. Low and concealed.

CALL
Distinct, low, piping 'phew'.

RESIDENT/VISITOR
Resident.

black cap and face

stubby black bill

white rump

rosy red breast

♂

QUICK ID
- Distinctive black head and bill
- White rump flash in flight
- Unusual rosy red breast of male
- Puffed feathers, swaying mating display

BEST TIME TO SPOT

	JAN	FEB	MAR	APR	MAY	JUN	JUL	AUG	SEP	OCT	NOV	DEC

43

Was its breast and throat pinkish in colour? ◯

Was its bill blue-grey and stubby? ◯

Was its tail a notched shape? ◯

Did it have a blue-grey head? ◯

Caterpillars are a favourite food of chaffinches, and make a perfect protein-packed meal for growing chicks.

My observations

_____
_____
_____
_____
_____
_____
_____
_____
_____
_____
_____
_____
_____

my drawings and photos

Chaffinch
(Fringilla coelebs)

The chaffinch is one of Britain's most common and popular garden birds. It rarely strays over a 5 kilometre radius of its nest. It is found everywhere, from open commons and gardens to woods and farmland. A very bold visitor to the bird table, it enthusiastically consumes scraps, seeds and berries, and can become quite tame. The chaffinch is sociable and roosts in groups in hedges. In winter it forages in the company of bramblings, sparrows greenfinches, and yellowhammers. The female is the main nest-builder, though the male brings some materials. She does most of the hatching, but both parents feed the young.

SIZE
Length 15 cm, Weight 19–23 g

COLOUR
MALE Grey head. Chestnut back. Pink-brown face and breast. White wing bars and outer tail feathers. Olive-green rump.
FEMALE Olive-brown head and back. Pale pink breast.
WINTER DIFFERENCES None.

NEST
Carefully woven from moss, grass, roots, camouflaged with lichens and spiders' webs. Tree fork, hedgerow or thick bush.

CALL
'Chwink' repeated. 'Choop' in flight.

RESIDENT/VISITOR
Resident, with many winter visitors from Europe.

grey head

bands of white on wings

brown tail

pink breast

♂

QUICK ID
- Grey cap of male with pink-brown face and breast
- Double white wing bars in flight
- 'Choop' flight call in winter flocks
- Olive-green rump in flight

BEST TIME TO SPOT

	JAN	FEB	MAR	APR	MAY	JUN	JUL	AUG	SEP	OCT	NOV	DEC
6												
5												
4												
3												
2												
1												
0												

Did it have a crimson-red face? ◯

Was there a yellow patch on its wing? ◯

Did it have a tinkling voice? ◯

Was its bill fine and pointed? ◯

My observations

_____
_____
_____
_____
_____
_____
_____
_____
_____
_____
_____
_____
_____

The long bill of the goldfinch, with its slender and sharp tip, is perfect for extracting the small seeds from a prickly thistle head.

my drawings and photos

Goldfinch
(Carduelis carduelis)

The goldfinch stands out amongst other garden birds for the sheer brilliance and contrasts of its colouring. It is sometimes known as the 'thistle finch' because it has a great fondness for certain plants such as thistles, dandelions and teazels. It flutters around their seed heads, delicately extracting the seeds with its sharply pointed beak. The goldfinch rarely comes to the bird table, but may be tempted by seeds and strings of peanuts. In autumn it sometimes teams up with redpolls and siskins to forage for seeds. It also eats small insects. Gardens, wastelands, orchards and roadsides are the goldfinch's main feeding grounds.

SIZE
Length 12 cm, Weight 14–17 g

COLOUR
MALE Black cap, white cheeks, throat and underparts. Brilliant red face. Black tail and wings. Bright yellow wing band. Brown back.
FEMALE Similar to male
WINTER DIFFERENCES None.

NEST
Roots, grass, moss, lichen, lined with plant down or wool. Placed at end of tree branch or in a dense hedge.

CALL
'Swit-wit-wit' perched or in flight.

RESIDENT/VISITOR
Resident.

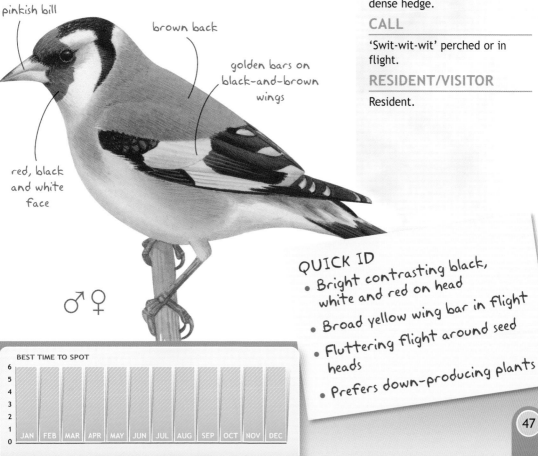

pinkish bill

brown back

golden bars on black-and-brown wings

red, black and white face

♂ ♀

QUICK ID
• Bright contrasting black, white and red on head
• Broad yellow wing bar in flight
• Fluttering flight around seed heads
• Prefers down-producing plants

BEST TIME TO SPOT

	JAN	FEB	MAR	APR	MAY	JUN	JUL	AUG	SEP	OCT	NOV	DEC

Was it quite a stocky bird? ◯

Did it have a thick bill? ◯

Was its upper plumage olive-green? ◯

Were its underparts yellow? ◯

In the summer, a male greenfinch has colourful plumage, but juveniles are mostly dull, with a speckled breast.

My observations

_____
_____
_____
_____
_____
_____
_____
_____
_____
_____
_____
_____
_____

my drawings and photos

Greenfinch

(Carduelis chloris)

The greenfinch is a common garden visitor, and is particularly keen on sunflower seeds and peanuts. It likes to feed with other birds, and moves in groups in trees and on the ground. A stocky bird, the greenfinch has a strong bill that it uses to tackle tough seeds. It has a varied diet that includes berries and buds, as well as insects such as ants and aphids. It can become quite aggressive if there is competition for food, and often drives other birds away from favourite food sources such as peanut feeders. It enjoys garden berries such as cotoneaster and yew.

SIZE

Length 14.5 cm, Weight 25–31 g

COLOUR

MALE Olive-green upper plumage, with a lighter, more yellow rump. Brighter yellow in tail and wings. Upper wing surfaces grey-green.
FEMALE Duller, with less yellow showing.
WINTER DIFFERENCES Brown tips to green plumage in winter.

NEST

Woven twigs and moss, lined with roots, hair and feathers. In hedgerows and evergreen bushes.

CALL

Drawn-out 'tswee'.

RESIDENT/VISITOR

Resident. Some visiting migrants come from Europe in autumn, departing again in spring.

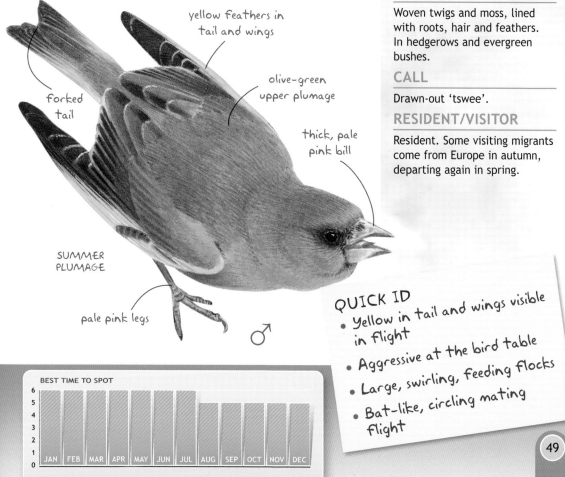

yellow feathers in tail and wings

forked tail

olive-green upper plumage

thick, pale pink bill

SUMMER PLUMAGE

pale pink legs

♂

QUICK ID
- Yellow in tail and wings visible in flight
- Aggressive at the bird table
- Large, swirling, feeding flocks
- Bat-like, circling mating flight

BEST TIME TO SPOT

	JAN	FEB	MAR	APR	MAY	JUN	JUL	AUG	SEP	OCT	NOV	DEC

Were its upperparts bright yellow? ◯

Did it have a black cap? ◯

Did it have a V-notch tail? ◯

Did it have streaked flanks? ◯

The male siskin (left) has bold colours and patterning. Females and this juvenile (right) have a more streaky, washed-out appearance.

My observations

_____
_____
_____
_____
_____
_____
_____
_____
_____
_____
_____
_____
_____

my drawings and photos

Siskin
(Carduelis spinus)

The siskin likes to live in coniferous woods but will nest in pine trees in the garden. At one time, resident siskins lived mostly in Scotland and Ireland, but the species has now spread further south in Britain due to an increase in conifer plantations. The siskin is mainly a seed-eater, and clings to twigs as it extracts them. In the garden it happily eats peanuts from the bird feeder, which it perhaps mistakes for pine cones. In winter, the siskin forages with redpolls through the top branches of spruce, birch, larch and alder trees.

SIZE
Length 12 cm, Weight 12–18 g

COLOUR
MALE Yellow-green back, paler underparts. Yellow rump, wing bar, eye stripe, sides of tail. Brown-streaked flanks. Black crown and chin.
FEMALE Duller. Less yellow. No black on head.
WINTER DIFFERENCES None.

NEST
Twigs and moss. Usually at the end of a conifer branch.

CALL
Squeaky 'tzy-zi'. Wheezy 'tsewi' in flight.

RESIDENT/VISITOR
Mainly a winter visitor from Scandinavia and the Baltic, but resident populations are increasing.

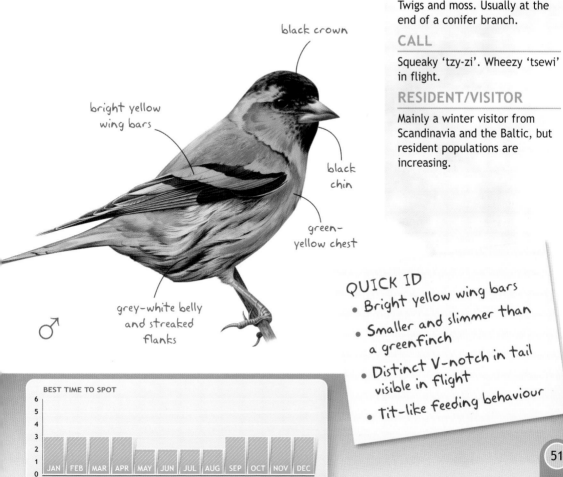

black crown

bright yellow wing bars

black chin

green-yellow chest

grey-white belly and streaked flanks

♂

QUICK ID
- Bright yellow wing bars
- Smaller and slimmer than a greenfinch
- Distinct V-notch in tail visible in flight
- Tit-like feeding behaviour

BEST TIME TO SPOT

JAN	FEB	MAR	APR	MAY	JUN	JUL	AUG	SEP	OCT	NOV	DEC

Did it have a black bib? ◯

Were its upperparts
streaked brown and black? ◯

Did it twitter? ◯

Did it have a grey crown? ◯

In wet countries, sparrows bathe in water to clean their plumage. They ruffle their feathers and spread their wings out to dry.

My observations

my drawings and photos

House sparrow

(Passer domesticus)

The house sparrow is the street urchin of the bird world and goes around in noisy gangs looking for food. It turns up wherever food might be available, from gardens and wasteland to farms and railways. It feeds on wild seeds, spilled grain, insects, scraps – anything. In winter the house sparrow finds both food and warmth in farm pens and stables. It can crowd out other birds at feeding sites, though its numbers are currently in decline. This little bird has learnt useful bird table techniques such as hovering and hanging upside down to get at food in suspended feeders. The house sparrow is a successful survivor that has spread across the world.

SIZE

Length 14.5 cm, Weight 22–31 g

COLOUR

MALE Grey crown. Red-brown border and nape. Pale grey cheeks merging into breast and underparts. Black around eye and into throat. Wings warm brown with black markings. White cheeks in breeding plumage.
FEMALE Duller. Paler back. No facial black. Pale eye band.
WINTER DIFFERENCES Bill is yellow-brown in winter and black in summer.

NEST

Untidy – straw and grass lined with feathers. In holes and crevices in buildings, also in trees and hedgerows. Often in colonies.

CALL

Loud 'cheep'. Constant twittering.

RESIDENT/VISITOR

Resident.

black eye stripe and throat patch

grey cap

chestnut brown plumage on back is darkly streaked

grey breast

WINTER PLUMAGE

♂

QUICK ID
- Grey crown on male
- Strong contrast between male and female
- White wing bar in flight
- Quarrelsome groups always on the move

BEST TIME TO SPOT

JAN	FEB	MAR	APR	MAY	JUN	JUL	AUG	SEP	OCT	NOV	DEC

6
5
4
3
2
1
0

Did it have a white moustache? ◯

Was its collar white? ◯

Was its head black? ◯

Did it fly in a short, jerky way? ◯

In the summer, male reed buntings have black-and-white heads. Males find a low perch and sing loudly to attract females.

My observations

_____
_____
_____
_____
_____
_____
_____
_____
_____
_____
_____
_____
_____
_____

my drawings and photos

Reed bunting
(Emberiza schoeniclus)

True to its name, the reed bunting is a bird of the wetlands. However it has now spread into some drier habitats. In the winter it leaves reed beds, marshes and upland areas, and moves to the fields. Here it looks for seeds and insects alongside finches and other buntings, like the yellowhammer. If threatened by approaching danger, the reed bunting pretends to be injured, crawling along with wings half-spread, leading the threat away from its nest. Because it is primarily a ground feeder, it is in danger of starvation when there is snow cover, and increasingly visits gardens in the winter for food.

SIZE
Length 15.5 cm, Weight 19 g

COLOUR
MALE Black head and throat. White collar, underparts and moustache. Chestnut back and wings with dark markings. Brown-and-grey tail with white outer feathers.

FEMALE Brown head. Pale eyebrow and moustache. Buff underparts. Back and wings ruddier than male.

WINTER DIFFERENCES Head and throat turn grey-brown.

NEST
Lined with leaves, grass, moss, and hair. On vegetation in marshy ground.

CALL
Loud 'tseek', and metallic 'chink'.

RESIDENT/VISITOR
Resident, but many continental reed buntings winter in Britain.

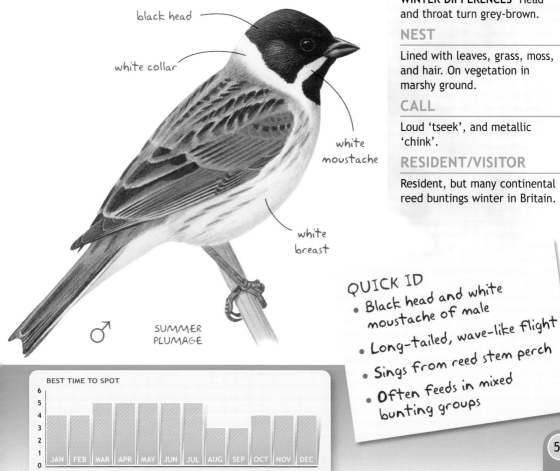

black head

white collar

white moustache

white breast

♂ SUMMER PLUMAGE

QUICK ID
- Black head and white moustache of male
- Long-tailed, wave-like flight
- Sings from reed stem perch
- Often feeds in mixed bunting groups

BEST TIME TO SPOT

JAN	FEB	MAR	APR	MAY	JUN	JUL	AUG	SEP	OCT	NOV	DEC
4	4	5	5	5	5	2	2	4	5	4	4

Did it have a
sharp, persistent call? ◯

Were its head, throat and breast grey? ◯

Were its upperparts dark-
streaked and its back brown? ◯

Was its bill thin? ◯

My observations

_____
_____
_____
_____
_____
_____
_____
_____
_____
_____
_____
_____
_____

Dunnocks are often chosen by cuckoos to incubate
and rear their chicks. Despite the size difference,
the adult dunnocks feed the cuckoo chicks.

my drawings and photos

Dunnock
(Prunella modularis)

Also known, incorrectly, as the hedge sparrow, the dunnock is not related to sparrows. It is a quiet and furtive bird, and creeps, mouse-like, along hedges and under bushes as it seeks the caterpillars, spiders and insects on which it feeds. In winter the dunnock is attracted to the garden bird table, but it is more hesitant than many other birds. It also carries out insect searches in crop fields, copses and along roadsides. The dunnock is found all over the British Isles except for the most northerly Scottish islands. It is often chosen as an unwitting foster parent by cuckoos.

SIZE
Length 14.5 cm, Weight 20–22 g

COLOUR
MALE Brown, dark-streaked back, cheeks and top of head. Grey mask and breast. Buff flanks.
FEMALE Same as male.
WINTER DIFFERENCES None.

NEST
Moss, wool, grass and hair. In hedges, bushes, woodpiles.

CALL
High 'tsieh'. Flight call is 'di-di-di'.

RESIDENT/VISITOR
Mainly resident, though some birds move southwards in autumn, and some even cross the Channel.

speckled feathers on back

thin, sharp bill

blue-grey throat, breast and eye stripe

♂ ♀

pink legs

QUICK ID
- Thin bill for eatng insects (unlike sparrow)
- Hops slowly, hunched close to ground
- Often seen in a trio of two males and one female
- Several birds may perform wing-waving display together

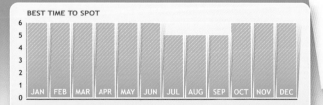

BEST TIME TO SPOT

| JAN | FEB | MAR | APR | MAY | JUN | JUL | AUG | SEP | OCT | NOV | DEC |

Did it have a crimson-red crown? ◯

Did it have a yellow rump? ◯

Was its moustache red and black? ◯

Was its call loud and like laughter? ◯

My observations

_____
_____
_____
_____
_____
_____
_____
_____
_____
_____
_____
_____

Female green woodpeckers lay between five and seven eggs, between May and July. The chicks hatch about three weeks later.

my drawings and photos

Green woodpecker
(Picus viridis)

The handsome green woodpecker lives in woodlands and parklands, and is Britain's largest woodpecker. It is a shy but noisy bird, and is unmistakable, especially in flight, with its bold colouring. Also unmistakable is its raucous 'yaffle' – a loud cry resembling hysterical laughter. It uses its long, pointed bill to excavate its nest-hole and to dig for ants, its main food. The ants stick to the woodpecker's long, sticky tongue. In the garden it is more likely to drill the lawn for ants than approach the bird table. When ants' nests are frozen hard, it has been known to bore into beehives.

SIZE
Length 30–33 cm, Weight 190 g

COLOUR
MALE Crimson crown and neck. Green back and wings. Yellow rump. Black face, black-and-red moustache. Grey outer wing feathers barred white and green. Grey-green undersides. Long, grey tail.
FEMALE Similar, but no red moustache.
WINTER DIFFERENCES None.

NEST
Bored in soft or rotting wood, vertical chamber with horizontal entrance. Wood chips cover base.

CALL
Loud laughing 'gluck-gluck-gluck'.

RESIDENT/VISITOR
Resident.

crimson-red crown and nape

bright green back and wings

black-and-red moustache

green-grey underparts

♂

QUICK ID
- Red, green and black colouring
- Laughing call
- Low, dipping flight
- Pointed bill, long tail feathers

BEST TIME TO SPOT

	JAN	FEB	MAR	APR	MAY	JUN	JUL	AUG	SEP	OCT	NOV	DEC

Did it have a black crown? ◯

Was the nape of its neck red? ◯

Were there bold white markings on its black back? ◯

Were its undertail feathers bright red? ◯

The juvenile (left) has a red cap on its head. This will disappear as the bird moults. The female (right) has a black cap, but no red nape like the male.

My observations

_____
_____
_____
_____
_____
_____
_____
_____
_____
_____
_____
_____
_____
_____

my drawings and photos

Great spotted woodpecker

(Dendrocopos major)

The most common woodpecker in Britain, the great spotted woodpecker is more likely to be seen in gardens than the green woodpecker, and is very partial to fat and peanuts. It is also known to take young birds, such as blue tits, out of nest boxes. The great spotted woodpecker gets most of its food by pecking at bark and rotten wood to extract insects and their larvae. It has also been seen wedging nuts into bark crevices, then cracking them with its beak. It defines its territory by 'drumming' – striking a branch with its bill in short bursts of rapid blows, a sound that can be heard over long distances.

SIZE
Length 22–23 cm, Weight 80 g

COLOUR
MALE Black cap and collar. Crimson nape and white cheeks. Black back and wings with white patches and white barred primary feathers. Crimson undertail.
FEMALE No red nape.
WINTER DIFFERENCES None.

NEST
A cavity freshly hollowed out each year, usually in a dead tree or stump.

CALL
'Tchik' repeated.

RESIDENT/VISITOR
Resident.

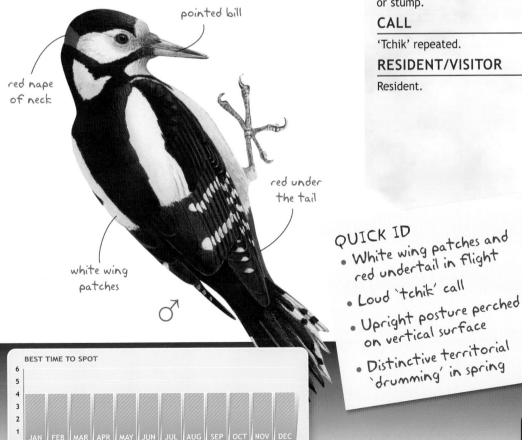

pointed bill

red nape of neck

red under the tail

white wing patches

♂

QUICK ID
- White wing patches and red undertail in flight
- Loud 'tchik' call
- Upright posture perched on vertical surface
- Distinctive territorial 'drumming' in spring

BEST TIME TO SPOT

	JAN	FEB	MAR	APR	MAY	JUN	JUL	AUG	SEP	OCT	NOV	DEC

6
5
4
3
2
1
0

Was the bird very small, almost sparrow-sized? ◯

Was it mainly black and white in colour? ◯

Was the crown bright red? ◯

Was it an agile climber? ◯

My observations

These woodpeckers chip insects out from the bark to eat, or feed their young. They use their tails as props when they perch.

my drawings and photos

Lesser spotted woodpecker
(Dendrocopos minor)

The lesser spotted woodpecker is about the size of a sparrow. Its colouring is like the great spotted woodpecker's but arranged differently. It is a shy bird, hunting insects out of sight in high branches. It 'drums' on bark to mark its territory. Unlike other woodpeckers, it joins winter feeding flocks of mixed tits. It is hardly ever seen at the bird table, approaching it very nervously if at all. It is normally only seen in England and Wales.

SIZE
Length 13–14 cm, Weight 20 g

COLOUR
MALE Red crown. Black nape, moustache stripes, back and tail. White face, brownish-white underparts, broad white wing bars.
FEMALE Less bright, and with whitish crown.
WINTER DIFFERENCES None.

NEST
Excavated by both birds in rotten wood up to 25 m above the ground. Very small entry hole – 3 cm wide.

CALL
'Kee-kee-kee'. Weak 'tchik'.

RESIDENT/VISITOR
Resident.

red crown

black-and-white wings

short, grey, thin bill

RARE

♂

QUICK ID
- Bright red crown of male
- Bold white wing bars
- Fluttering to remain in position when feeding
- Woodpecker shape, tiny size

BEST TIME TO SPOT

6												
5												
4												
3												
2												
1												
0	JAN	FEB	MAR	APR	MAY	JUN	JUL	AUG	SEP	OCT	NOV	DEC

Was this bird near water? ◯

Did you see it dive for fish? ◯

Was it carrying something in its bill? ◯

Was it small and fast? ◯

My observations

When a kingfisher dives for a meal, it opens its bill slightly. Its delicate eyes are protected by a membrane.

my drawings and photos

Kingfisher

(Alcedo atthis)

Kingfishers are easy to recognise, due to their electric-blue plumage. These birds are very shy, and flit between trees so quickly that they are hard to spot in dappled shade. Kingfishers perch on branches that overhang slow-flowing rivers, and dive headfirst into the water to catch food. They mostly eat small fish, but will also catch tadpoles, shrimps and insects. Caught fish are taken back to a tree, and hit against a branch until dead. They are swallowed whole. A kingfisher needs to eat its own bodyweight in food every day.

SIZE
Length 16 cm, Weight 40 g

COLOUR
MALE Bright blue plumage on the upper body and ruddy orange beneath. The head is blue and barred, with a white-and-orange cheek patch. Black bill.

FEMALE Similar to the male, but the black bill has a red base.

WINTER DIFFERENCES None.

NEST
Burrow, dug into soft earth near water.

CALL
Loud calls of 'cheeee'. Trills in spring.

RESIDENT/VISITOR
Resident.

barring on top of head

white-and-orange cheeks

long, strong bill

short red legs

♀

QUICK ID
- Electric-blue feathers
- Long, pointed bill
- Big head, small body
- White cheek and chin

BEST TIME TO SPOT

JAN	FEB	MAR	APR	MAY	JUN	JUL	AUG	SEP	OCT	NOV	DEC

Did it have something in its bill? ○

Was it flying silently? ○

Was it in open country? ○

Did you see it during the day? ○

My observations

_____
_____
_____
_____
_____
_____
_____
_____
_____
_____
_____
_____

The legs of the barn owl are very long, helping the owl to grab prey in the undergrowth. Prey is killed using the talons rather than the beak.

my drawings and photos

Barn owl

(Tyto alba)

Although barn owls are mostly nocturnal – active at night – they often hunt around sunset and sunrise. During the winter they may even fly during the day, looking for voles, mice and rats. Barn owls catch their prey with sharp talons and swallow animals whole. Body parts they cannot digest are regurgitated as dark pellets that contain teeth, bones and fur. Up to seven small, white eggs are laid in a nest, usually in the spring, but most of the chicks die in their first year. Barn owls can live to the age of 12 or more.

SIZE

Length 34 cm, Weight 300 g

COLOUR

MALE Buff-coloured back, flecked with dark spots near tail. White underparts and face.
FEMALE Same as male.
WINTER DIFFERENCES None.

NEST

No nest. Eggs are laid on ledges in farm buildings, inside haystacks, tree hollows and owl nest boxes.

CALL

Hissing, shrieking, snoring and a 'hi-wit' call.

RESIDENT/VISITOR

Resident.

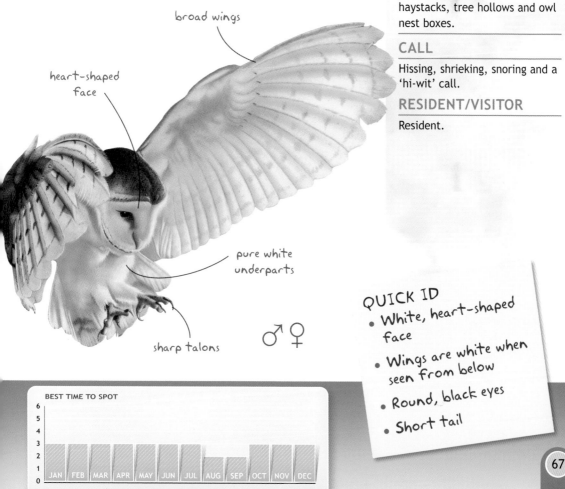

broad wings

heart-shaped face

pure white underparts

sharp talons

♂ ♀

QUICK ID
- White, heart-shaped face
- Wings are white when seen from below
- Round, black eyes
- Short tail

BEST TIME TO SPOT

	6	5	4	3	2	1	0
JAN	FEB	MAR	APR	MAY	JUN	JUL	AUG	SEP	OCT	NOV	DEC

Did it have a large rounded head? ◯

Did it have a distinctive facial disc? ◯

Was its tail short and square? ◯

Was its bill hooked? ◯

My observations

_____

_____

_____

_____

_____

_____

_____

_____

_____

_____

_____

_____

_____

Primarily a nocturnal bird, the tawny owl is rarely seen during the day, preferring to spend its time sleeping in its roost.

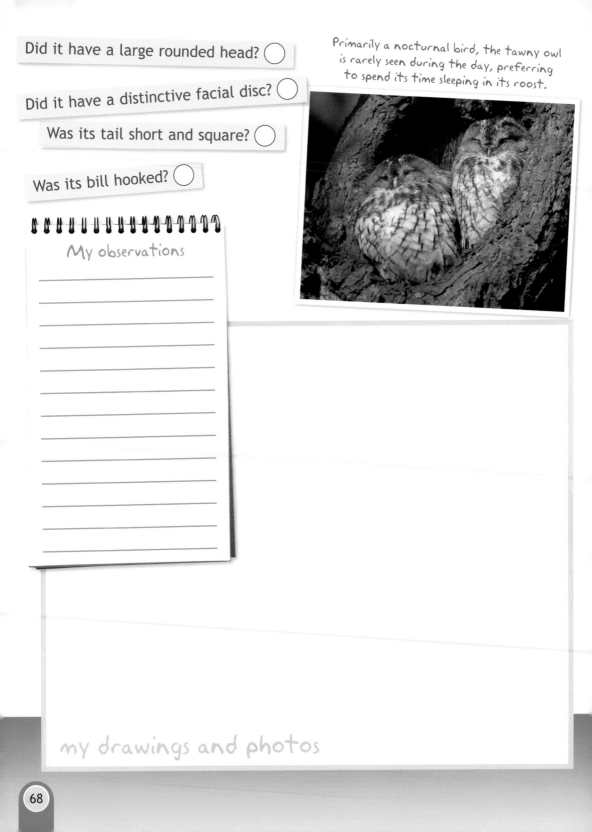

my drawings and photos

Tawny owl
(Strix aluco)

This woodland predator is now also found in parks and gardens. Where once it hunted small mammals, in urban areas it often hunts small birds. Any appearance at the bird table is in pursuit of other birds. It uses a different perch each night, usually high up, and from here it calls to contact mates and warn off rivals. It flies in silence, its wing-beats muffled by downy edges on its wing feathers. As well as mammals and birds, the tawny owl feeds on insects, frogs and newts. In cities, it may catch bats such as pipistrelles and noctules.

SIZE

Length 37–39 cm,
Weight 350–500 g

COLOUR

MALE Red-brown to grey back. Buff underparts, with distinct, dark streaking. Grey-brown facial disc. Black eyes.
FEMALE Same as male.
WINTER DIFFERENCES None.

NEST

Hole in tree. Also uses old crow and heron nests, squirrel dreys, holes in farm buildings. No nesting material used.

CALL

Female 'ke-wick'. Male 'hoo hoooo'.

RESIDENT/VISITOR

Resident.

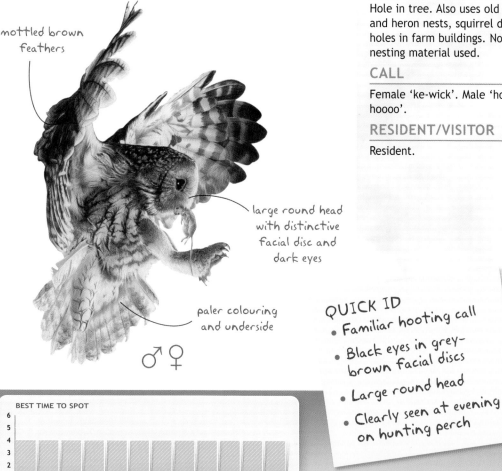

mottled brown feathers

large round head with distinctive facial disc and dark eyes

paler colouring and underside

♂♀

QUICK ID
• Familiar hooting call
• Black eyes in grey-brown facial discs
• Large round head
• Clearly seen at evening on hunting perch

BEST TIME TO SPOT

	JAN	FEB	MAR	APR	MAY	JUN	JUL	AUG	SEP	OCT	NOV	DEC

6
5
4
3
2
1
0

Were its upperparts light brown? ◯

Did it have a warbling voice? ◯

Were its underparts buff-coloured? ◯

Was its bill short and slender? ◯

My observations

_____
_____
_____
_____
_____
_____
_____
_____
_____
_____
_____
_____
_____

Garden warblers come to Britain to breed because they can find plenty of food for their growing chicks.

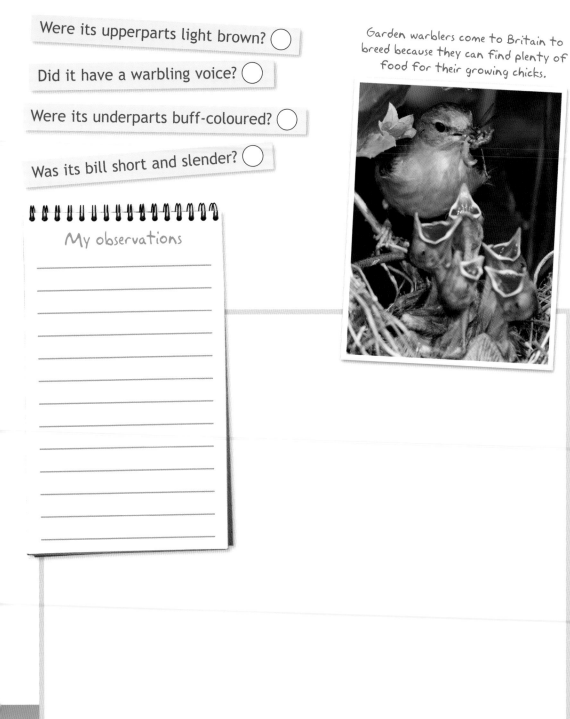

my drawings and photos

Garden warbler

(Sylvia borin)

The garden warbler is a summer visitor that could be easily overlooked with its bland, mousy colouring. But it has a glorious singing voice. Despite its name, it is rarely seen in any but the largest gardens, as it prefers to live in overgrown hedges, woodlands with thick undergrowth, and bushy commons. Related to the blackcap, and sharing its migration pattern, the garden warbler avoids competition with its relative by feeding at a lower level. It is an insect-eater, but also feeds on berries and fruit when insects are scarce in autumn.

SIZE

Length 13–15 cm
Weight 16–23 g

COLOUR

MALE Light-brown back. Paler buff underparts. Pale, narrow eye ring. Faint grey neck spot.
FEMALE Same as male.
WINTER DIFFERENCES None.

NEST

Cup-shaped, made of dry grass, lined with rootlets and hair. Low in bushes, including rhododendrons and brambles.

CALL

'Check-check'. Warbling, bubbling song with long phrases and pure tones.

RESIDENT/VISITOR

Summer visitor, arriving in April and returning to sub-Saharan Africa in late October.

small, slender bill

pale, narrow eye ring

olive brown plumage

♂ ♀

paler colour underneath

QUICK ID
- Short, square-ended tail visible in flight
- Smooth colouring lacking sharp contrasts
- Sustained warbling song with long phrases
- Compact, stocky build

BEST TIME TO SPOT

	JAN	FEB	MAR	APR	MAY	JUN	JUL	AUG	SEP	OCT	NOV	DEC

Did it look like a chiffchaff? ◯

Did it have a yellow eye stripe? ◯

Were its legs pale? ◯

Did it have a notch-shaped tail? ◯

My observations

Willow warblers use their long slender bills to pick up insects and they are so quick they can even catch flies in the air.

my drawings and photos

Willow warbler

(Phylloscopus trochilus)

Flying in from North Africa every spring, the willow warbler is one of the most commonly seen summer visitors to Europe. On its arrival in Britain it often refuels by feeding on insects found on flowering willows. The willow warbler is full of nervous energy, and is forever on the move, flicking its wings as it busily forages for insects. A fine singer, it sings its song from trees and bushes while working its way through foliage seeking insects, and while flying. When courting the female, the male perches near her and slowly waves one or both of his wings at her.

SIZE

Length 11 cm, Weight 6–10 g

COLOUR

MALE Olive-brown back. Yellow breast. Whitish underparts. Yellow stripe over eye. Dusky-coloured wing and tail feathers.
FEMALE Same as male.
WINTER DIFFERENCES None.

NEST

Half-dome shape, made of grass and lined with feathers. On the ground, beneath gorse bushes, in hedge banks.

CALL

'Hoo-id' – two syllables. Song – a falling sequence of clear notes.

RESIDENT/VISITOR

A summer visitor from North Africa, arriving in Britain in April, and returning there in September.

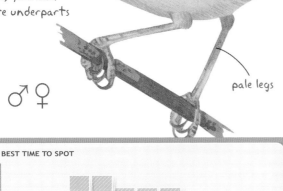

yellow eye stripe

olive-brown plumage

pale, yellowish-white underparts

♂ ♀

pale legs

QUICK ID
- Yellowish tones to plumage
- Yellow stripe over eye
- Sometimes flutters like a flycatcher when hunting
- Cascading, liquid song

BEST TIME TO SPOT

	JAN	FEB	MAR	APR	MAY	JUN	JUL	AUG	SEP	OCT	NOV	DEC

Was it rather like a willow warbler? ◯

Was its song a distinctive chiff-chaff call? ◯

Did it have a cream line above the eye and eye ring? ◯

Were its legs dark-coloured? ◯

Chiffchaffs look very similar to willow warblers, but they are a little smaller. They also bob their tails up and down.

My observations

_____
_____
_____
_____
_____
_____
_____
_____
_____
_____
_____
_____

my drawings and photos

Chiffchaff

(Phylloscopus collybita)

The chiffchaff is sometimes known as the 'leaf warbler' because of its excellent colour camouflage in foliage. It feeds mainly high up in trees, on caterpillars and tiny insects such as midges. The male arrives in this country before the female and lays claim to nesting territory with loud singing. The female hatches the young and looks after them with little or no help from the male. Chiffchaffs are rarely seen at the bird table, but only a minority overwinter here. Bird table food supplies may have influenced the increase in visitors such as the chiffchaff, and some have begun to stay all year round.

SIZE
Length 11 cm, Weight 6–9 g

COLOUR
MALE Brownish olive head and back. Grey-white underparts. Pale yellow breast. Cream line above eye and eye ring.
FEMALE Same as male.
WINTER DIFFERENCES None.

NEST
Dry grass, moss, leaves, feathers. On or near ground. Domed.

CALL
'Hweet'. Song – 'chiff-chaff' and variations, repeated.

RESIDENT/VISITOR
Visitor from around the Mediterranean. One of the first visiting songbirds to arrive in March. Some have become residents.

pale stripe over eye

olive brown plumage on back and head

thin, short bill

grey-white underparts

thin, dark legs

short wingtips

♂ ♀

QUICK ID
- Distinctive 'chiff-chaff' song
- Dark legs
- More often on the ground than the willow warbler
- Clear eye ring

BEST TIME TO SPOT

JAN	FEB	MAR	APR	MAY	JUN	JUL	AUG	SEP	OCT	NOV	DEC

Were its throat and breast greyish-brown? ◯

Did it have a black cap? ◯

Was its back brown? ◯

Was it greyish-brown underneath? ◯

Female blackcaps have red-brown caps and their bodies are browner. Juvenile females have yellowish caps.

My observations

_____
_____
_____
_____
_____
_____
_____
_____
_____
_____
_____
_____
_____
_____

my drawings and photos

Blackcap
(Sylvia atricapilla)

The blackcap belongs to the warbler family, and shares the warblers' talent for singing. In the spring it can be seen and heard from a high perch, often an oak tree. Blackcaps and garden warblers are often seen working their way through brambles and undergrowth together. Although mainly an insect-eater, the blackcap is an enthusiastic berry- and fruit-eater in the autumn. Increasing numbers of blackcaps are overwintering in Britain, and these are appearing at the bird table during winter months. In the garden the blackcap can be aggressive when competing for scraps, often frightening off much larger birds.

SIZE
Length 13–15 cm,
Weight 14–20 g

COLOUR
MALE Grey-brown back. Grey underparts. Distinctive black cap ending at eye level.
FEMALE Brown-buff underparts and red-brown cap.
WINTER DIFFERENCES None.

NEST
Grass, roots, hair lining. In thick undergrowth, brambles and bushes.

CALL
'Tak' when disturbed. Song – loud and warbling.

RESIDENT/VISITOR
Summer visitor from the Mediterranean and North Africa. Increasing number of winter residents.

black cap

grey-brown back

notched tail

♂

QUICK ID
- Male's black cap, ending at eye level
- Female's bright red-brown cap
- Aggressive bird table behaviour

BEST TIME TO SPOT

	JAN	FEB	MAR	APR	MAY	JUN	JUL	AUG	SEP	OCT	NOV	DEC
6												
5												
4												
3												
2												
1												
0												

Was its body torpedo-shaped? ◯

Was its tail short and forked? ◯

Was its voice like a
high-pitched scream? ◯

Was it similar to a swallow? ◯

My observations

_____
_____
_____
_____
_____
_____
_____
_____
_____
_____
_____
_____
_____

Swifts rarely perch, and usually only stop
flying when they visit their nests. They rarely
have more than three chicks.

my drawings and photos

Swift
(Apus apus)

The swifts we see and hear in our skies have probably been hatched here, but they spend over half of the year in Africa. The swift is an extraordinary bird, which spends practically all its life in the air. Living on flying insects and floating spiders caught in midair, the swift feeds, sleeps, and even sometimes mates on the wing. It lands to build its nest, lay and hatch its eggs, and care for the young until they leave the nest. When the young do finally leave the nest, they are likely to stay airborne for the next two or three years.

SIZE
Length 16.5 cm, Weight 45 g

COLOUR
MALE Dull brown all over, apart from light patch under chin.
FEMALE Same as male.
WINTER DIFFERENCES None.

NEST
Straw, feathers, plant-down collected in midair, bound together with saliva. Sited in holes in trees, caves, buildings. Will accept a suitable nest box.

CALL
Shrill 'swee-ree', emitted much of the time. Female call has higher pitch.

RESIDENT/VISITOR
Arrives in May from Africa. Leaves early August.

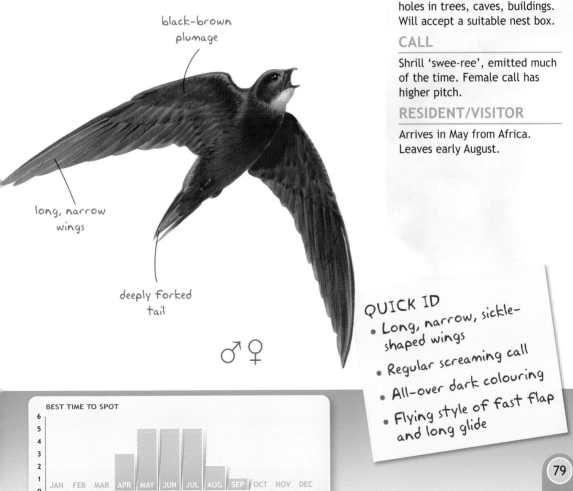

black-brown plumage

long, narrow wings

deeply forked tail

♂ ♀

QUICK ID
- Long, narrow, sickle-shaped wings
- Regular screaming call
- All-over dark colouring
- Flying style of fast flap and long glide

BEST TIME TO SPOT

| | JAN | FEB | MAR | APR | MAY | JUN | JUL | AUG | SEP | OCT | NOV | DEC |

Did it have a deeply forked tail? ◯

Was it flying acrobatically? ◯

Was the top of the
bird blue-black in colour? ◯

Were its wings long and angled? ◯

My observations

_____
_____
_____
_____
_____
_____
_____
_____
_____
_____
_____

Swallows devote the summer months
to breeding. They can have two or three
broods, each with up to six chicks.

my drawings and photos

Swallow

(Hirundo rustica)

Once a cliff-nester, the swallow now prefers to build its nest in and around human habitation. It is a low flier, skimming the surface of rivers and ponds to catch insects in its gaping bill, or snatch a drink on the wing. The swallow is a fine navigator, and often returns to the same nest site for several years. Unlike the swift, the swallow can perch without problems on wires and buildings. It rarely lands on the ground, except to collect mud for nest building. Swallows are social birds, and hundreds often roost together in reed beds. Swallows gathering on telephone wires before returning south are a familiar sight.

SIZE
Length 19 cm, Weight 20 g

COLOUR
MALE Dark, glossy blue upperparts, head and upper breast. Dark red forehead, chin and throat. White to creamy underparts.
FEMALE Similar to male, though a little duller.
WINTER DIFFERENCES None.

NEST
Shallow cup-shaped, mud and dry grass, cemented with saliva. On ledges and rafters in barns, stables and other buildings. Often in colonies.

CALL
'Tswit-tswit'. Alarm call is a high 'tswee'.

RESIDENT/VISITOR
A summer visitor, arriving as early as late March. Returns to sub-Saharan Africa in September or October.

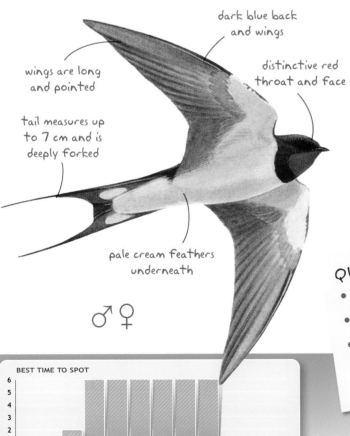

dark blue back and wings

wings are long and pointed

distinctive red throat and face

tail measures up to 7 cm and is deeply forked

pale cream feathers underneath

♂ ♀

QUICK ID
- Long tail streamers
- Red head and throat
- Dark blue breast band
- Low-level flight in straight lines

BEST TIME TO SPOT

JAN FEB MAR APR MAY JUN JUL AUG SEP OCT NOV DEC

Did it have a white chin and rump? ◯

Was its tail short and forked? ◯

Was its head blue-black? ◯

Were its wings black? ◯

When there is little rain in spring, house martins struggle to find mud to build nests, and cluster around any suitable puddles.

My observations

_____

_____

_____

_____

_____

_____

_____

_____

_____

_____

_____

_____

_____

_____

my drawings and photos

House martin
(Delichon urbica)

The house martin has developed a closer connection with human habitation than even the swallow. It builds its unique mud nest close under the eaves on the outsides of buildings. It is a social bird, and often nests in colonies. The house martin lives on a diet of flying insects caught in mid-air. It has a streamlined body and is a powerful and agile flier, though it flutters more than a swallow. It can land on the ground, where it collects mud for its nest-building. House martin pairs bring up two or three broods per year, and sometimes young birds from the first brood help to feed birds from later broods.

SIZE
Length 12.5 cm, Weight 18 g

COLOUR
MALE Blue-black above. White chin, throat, underparts and rump. Dark grey wings and tail. Short white leg feathers.
FEMALE Same as male.
WINTER DIFFERENCES None.

NEST
A mud-and-feathers cup with a small entrance hole, constructed under building eaves.

CALL
'Tsrr'. Alarm call 'sier-ier'.

RESIDENT/VISITOR
Summer visitor, arriving in April from sub-Saharan Africa, and returning in September or October.

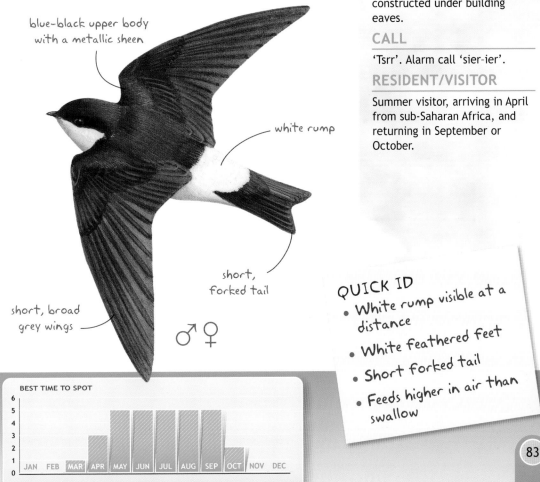

blue–black upper body with a metallic sheen

white rump

short, forked tail

short, broad grey wings

♂ ♀

QUICK ID
- White rump visible at a distance
- White feathered feet
- Short forked tail
- Feeds higher in air than swallow

BEST TIME TO SPOT

| | JAN | FEB | MAR | APR | MAY | JUN | JUL | AUG | SEP | OCT | NOV | DEC |

Did it run along the ground with its tail wagging? ◯

Did it have a long, notched tail? ◯

Was it black and white? ◯

Did it have a black bib? ◯

Wagtails wag their tails most when they feed. This behaviour may help them to flush out insects, which they can then catch.

My observations

my drawings and photos

Pied wagtail

(Motacilla alba)

The pied wagtail always seems to be in a hurry, running over the ground in fast bursts, stopping, wagging its tail up and down, then running on. All the time it is looking for insects, frequently stabbing at the ground or leaping into the air to capture a titbit. It rarely comes to the bird table, but will pick up what other birds have dropped on the ground. The pied wagtail is found across the country, and likes foraging at the edge of water where there is plenty of insect life. In the evening it flies to roost, with hundreds of others, in reeds and bushes.

SIZE

Length 18 cm, Weight 22 g

COLOUR

MALE White forehead and face. Black crown, throat, upper breast, back, tail. Outer wing and outer tail feathers white. Underparts white.
FEMALE Greyer back. Smaller bib.
WINTER DIFFERENCES Greyer back and white throat.

NEST

Cup-shaped, made of dry grass, and lined with rootlets and hair. Low in bushes, including rhododendrons, and brambles.

CALL

'Tu-reep' and 'tchisseek'.

RESIDENT/VISITOR

Resident, though some move further south in the country in winter, and some continue on as far as the Mediterranean.

black crown, throat and upper breast

white bars on wing feathers

long tail that constantly moves

white face

white feathers

SUMMER PLUMAGE ♂

QUICK ID
- Runs in short, fast bursts
- Tail wags up and down
- Wave-like, swooping flight
- Black-and-white plumage

BEST TIME TO SPOT

	JAN	FEB	MAR	APR	MAY	JUN	JUL	AUG	SEP	OCT	NOV	DEC

Was its breast speckled? ◯

Did it have a short, broad bill? ◯

Was it perched in an upright position? ◯

Did it have a streaked crown? ◯

The female spotted flytcatcher lays her eggs between June and August. This woodpile provides good camouflage for the nest.

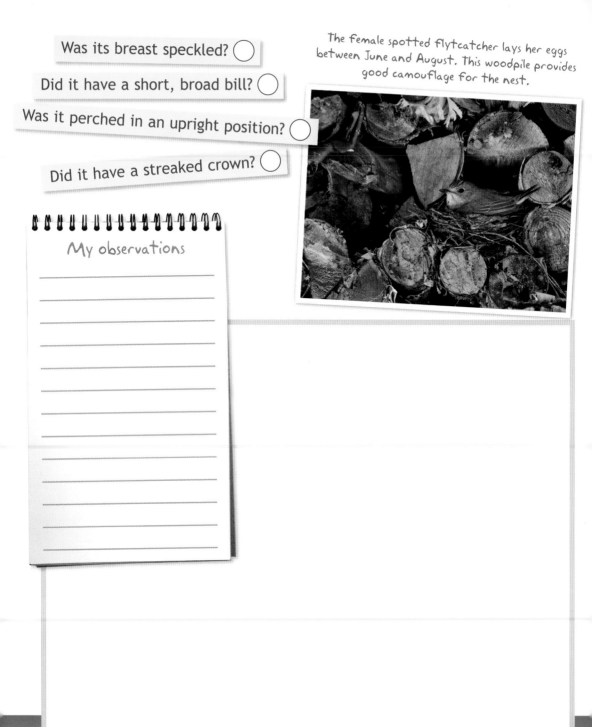

My observations

_____

_____

_____

_____

_____

_____

_____

_____

_____

_____

_____

_____

_____

my drawings and photos

Spotted flycatcher
(Muscicapa striata)

The spotted flycatcher eats any flying insects. When it catches something with a sting, it batters it against its perch until it is no longer a threat. Males and females usually feed separately, and hunting is done from a perch such as a stump. The spotted flycatcher is an ambush-hunter, sitting on its perch for long stretches, then suddenly darting off to seize a passing insect, returning to the perch to eat it. Its favourite hunting areas are wood margins and clearings, overgrown gardens, parkland and beside water, but its numbers are now in decline. It is often found near human habitation.

SIZE
Length 14 cm, Weight 15–16 g

COLOUR
MALE Grey-brown upper plumage. Off-white underparts with grey streaks. Streaked forehead and breast.
FEMALE Same as male.
WINTER DIFFERENCES None.

NEST
Untidy – moss, wool, hair, bound with cobwebs. On a ledge in creeper on wall or tree. On a bough or a beam. In an old nest of another bird.

CALL
'Tsee' and 'tzek-tuk-tuk'.

RESIDENT/VISITOR
Summer visitor, arriving in May from Africa, returning in July to September.

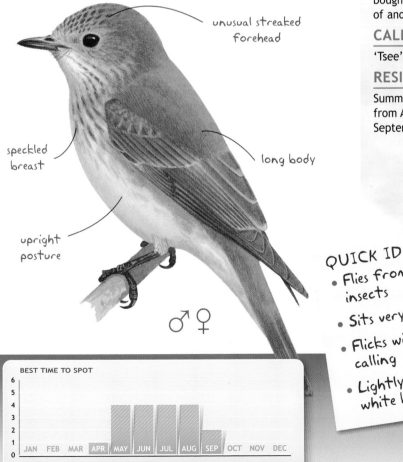

unusual streaked forehead

speckled breast

long body

upright posture

♂ ♀

QUICK ID
- Flies from perch to catch insects
- Sits very upright on perch
- Flicks wings and tail when calling
- Lightly streaked, off-white breast

BEST TIME TO SPOT

	JAN	FEB	MAR	APR	MAY	JUN	JUL	AUG	SEP	OCT	NOV	DEC
6												
5												
4												
3												
2												
1												
0												

Did it have a red face and breast? ◯

Did it have a high-pitched, sweet song? ◯

Was the rest of the bird light brown? ◯

Was its belly white? ◯

Young, or juvenile, robins lack the characteristic colour of their parents. The dull plumage allows them to hide from predators.

My observations

my drawings and photos

Robin

(Erithacus rubecula)

Probably Britain's most easily recognised bird, the robin is perfectly at home in the garden. It is famous for boldly coming close to anyone digging, in the hope of catching worms and grubs that are dug up. The robin sings to establish its territorial boundaries, and attract mates. It defends its territory with extreme aggression, and has even been known to fight to the death. In very harsh weather robins may observe a temporary truce, and you could see several feeding together at the bird table. Unafraid of humans, they rapidly become almost hand-tame when provided with regular food.

SIZE

Length 14 cm, Weight 16–22 g

COLOUR

MALE Light brown crown, back, tail and wings. Face and breast bright orange-red. Undersides white with buff tinge, with bands of white extending round the red breast, up and over the eyes.
FEMALE Same as male.
WINTER DIFFERENCES None.

NEST

Domed, made of grass, wool, moss, hair. In hole in bank or wall. Sometimes in sheds, in old buckets and other containers.

CALL

'Tik-tik'. Sweet, high-pitched twittery song.

RESIDENT/VISITOR

Resident. Joined by paler-coloured visitors from northern Europe in winter.

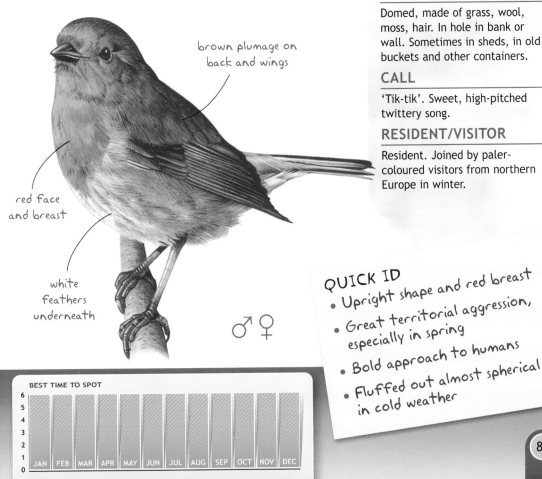

brown plumage on back and wings

red face and breast

white feathers underneath

♂ ♀

QUICK ID
• Upright shape and red breast
• Great territorial aggression, especially in spring
• Bold approach to humans
• Fluffed out almost spherical in cold weather

BEST TIME TO SPOT

6											
5											
4											
3											
2											
1											
0	JAN	FEB	MAR	APR	MAY	JUN	JUL	AUG	SEP	OCT	NOV	DEC

Was it flitting and hopping about? ◯

Did it have a cocked tail? ◯

Did it have barred markings on its back, wings and tail? ◯

Was it small and round? ◯

When a little wren sings it perks up its tail, puffs out its wings and opens its long bill wide. The resulting song can be heard from afar.

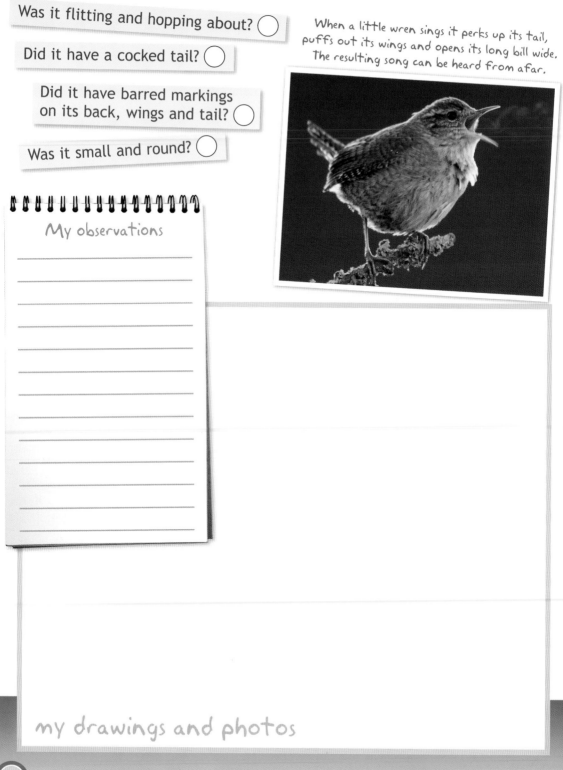

My observations

my drawings and photos

Wren
(Troglodytes troglodytes)

The tiny wren features in many folk tales. It is a resident species and is found in most terrains except the centres of large cities. This common garden bird has fast movements and a whirring flight. The male makes several nests at the beginning of the breeding season, and the female chooses which one to line and use for laying her eggs. The wren eats mainly larvae and spiders as well as some seeds. Like other very small birds, it sometimes nests with others in winter to keep warm. More than 60 have been known to cram into a single nestbox. As much as 70 percent of the wren population may fail to survive a harsh winter.

SIZE
Length 9.5 cm, Weight 9 g

COLOUR
MALE Russet-brown back, with darker bars. Wings, tail and flanks distinctly barred. Lighter underparts. Cream stripe over eye.
FEMALE Same as male.
WINTER DIFFERENCES None.

NEST
Moss, grass, bracken, local materials. Domed shape. In banks, piles of wood, thickets, walls, tree roots.

CALL
'Tek-tek' and 'tsrr'. Loud, trilling song – some notes too high for human hearing.

RESIDENT/VISITOR
Resident.

faint eye stripe

short, upright tail

narrow bill with downward pointing tip

barred pattern on wings and tail

♂ ♀

QUICK ID
- Tail cocked vertically most of the time
- tiny size, round shape
- Mouse-like movements through hedge bottoms
- Thin, insect-eater's bill

BEST TIME TO SPOT

JAN	FEB	MAR	APR	MAY	JUN	JUL	AUG	SEP	OCT	NOV	DEC

6
5
4
3
2
1
0

Was it a large bird? ◯

Did it have a pink breast? ◯

Was there a shiny
patch on its neck? ◯

Did it make a repetitive 'coo' call? ◯

Woodpigeons can swoop and soar thanks to
their large wings. The flight feathers are
spread out to increase surface area.

My observations

_____
_____
_____
_____
_____
_____
_____
_____
_____
_____
_____
_____
_____
_____

my drawings and photos

Woodpigeon
(Columba palumbus)

The impressive size of the woodpigeon clearly marks it out from others in the dove and pigeon family. Its take-off is a startling clatter of wings, and it is a powerful flier. With populations in both town and country, the woodpigeon is mainly a ground feeder, but it prefers an environment with plenty of trees in which to perch and nest. It feeds on plant material, seeds and berries, and crops such as peas and beans. It will visit the bird table, but is a nuisance in the vegetable garden, where it specializes in devouring young plants of the cabbage family, as well as soft fruit.

SIZE
Length 41 cm, Weight 500 g

COLOUR
MALE Blue-grey head. Greeny-blue nape. White patches on side of neck. Pale salmon throat and breast. Buff wings with a white band. Dark grey outer wing feathers.
FEMALE Similar to male.
WINTER DIFFERENCES None.

NEST
A few twigs. In hedgerows, trees, old nests. Also ledges on town buildings.

CALL
'Coo-COOO-coo, coo-coo'.

RESIDENT/VISITOR
Resident.

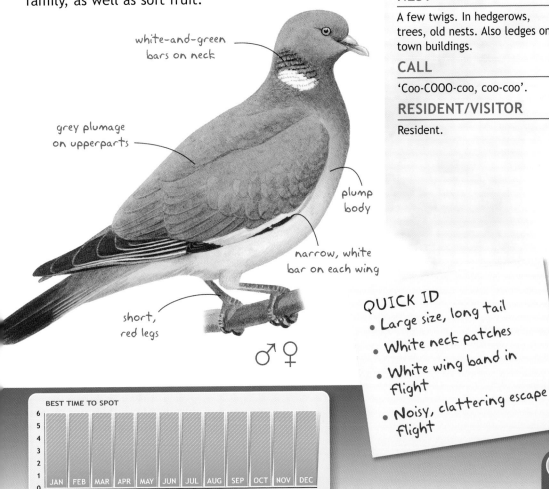

white-and-green bars on neck

grey plumage on upperparts

plump body

narrow, white bar on each wing

short, red legs

♂ ♀

QUICK ID
• Large size, long tail
• White neck patches
• White wing band in flight
• Noisy, clattering escape flight

BEST TIME TO SPOT

	JAN	FEB	MAR	APR	MAY	JUN	JUL	AUG	SEP	OCT	NOV	DEC

Was it pigeon or hawk-like in appearance? ◯

Was its song a repeated 'coo-cooo' sound? ◯

Did it look ungainly when perching? ◯

Did it have a long tail? ◯

The cuckoo egg is obvious to us, but the nest-owner does not recognise it as any different to its own smaller eggs.

My observations

_____
_____
_____
_____
_____
_____
_____
_____
_____
_____
_____
_____
_____

my drawings and photos

Cuckoo

(Cuculus canorus)

The cuckoo is known for its very distinctive call, and is often thought to be the harbinger of spring. The female watches a pair of small birds building their nest and at the moment they are absent will visit it, remove one of their eggs and lay her own single egg in its place. The unsuspecting small birds find themselves the parents to a huge and hungry cuckoo chick. Cuckoos are a widespread summer visitor in the British Isles, but their numbers are now in decline.

SIZE

Length 30–33 cm,
Weight 106–133 g

COLOUR

MALE Grey back and head.
Barred white underparts.
FEMALE As male.
WINTER DIFFERENCES None.

NEST

Uses nest of other smaller birds.

CALL

'Coo-cooo' from male, chuckling bubbling call from female.

RESIDENT/VISITOR

Summer visitor.

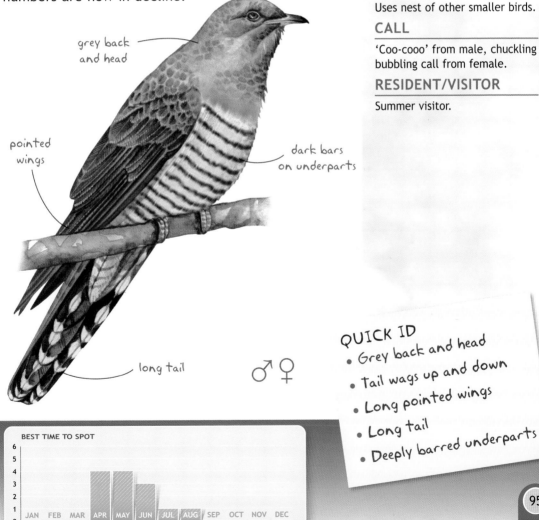

grey back and head

pointed wings

dark bars on underparts

long tail

♂ ♀

QUICK ID
- Grey back and head
- Tail wags up and down
- Long pointed wings
- Long tail
- Deeply barred underparts

BEST TIME TO SPOT

	JAN	FEB	MAR	APR	MAY	JUN	JUL	AUG	SEP	OCT	NOV	DEC
6												
5												
4												
3												
2												
1												
0												

Did it have a tail with a dark-banded tip? ◯

Was its breast pinkish? ◯

Did it have a turquoise-green neck patch? ◯

Did it have tiny, black wing bars? ◯

Stock doves often feed together, and can congregate in large numbers in the evening to roost in treetops.

My observations

_____
_____
_____
_____
_____
_____
_____
_____
_____
_____
_____
_____
_____

my drawings and photos

Stock dove

(Columba oenas)

More solitary than woodpigeons, stock doves can sometimes be seen feeding alongside them in the winter. Found everywhere in Britain except the extreme north of Scotland, the stock dove's habitats include woods, rocky coasts, dunes, cliffs and parkland. It occasionally eats snails and larvae, but most of its food is vegetable, including leaves, crops such as beans and corn, clover, seeds, buds and flowers. The stock dove has an impressive display flight in the breeding season when both male and female fly around in circles, gliding with raised wings, and performing wing 'clapping'. On the ground they go through bowing ceremonies.

SIZE

Length 32–34 cm,
Weight 290–330 g

COLOUR

MALE Purplish blue head, body and wings. Dark edges to wings, plus two small dark bars. Glossy turquoise-green nape. Rosy breast. Broad band at end of tail.
FEMALE Similar to male.
WINTER DIFFERENCES None.

NEST

Roots and twigs. In holes in trees, cliffs, caves, rabbit burrows. Sometimes no nesting material used.

CALL

'OOO-roo-oo'.

RESIDENT/VISITOR

Resident.

glossy turquoise-green neck

small wing bars

broad tail band

♂ ♀

QUICK ID
- Absence of any white on plumage
- Loud, rhythmic, booming call
- Two small wing bars and dark edges to wings
- Two black spots on wings seen in flight

BEST TIME TO SPOT

	JAN	FEB	MAR	APR	MAY	JUN	JUL	AUG	SEP	OCT	NOV	DEC
6												
5												
4												
3												
2												
1												
0												

Did it have a repeated 'coo-cooo-coo' call? ◯

Did it have a black collar, edged with white? ◯

Was its tail tipped with white underneath? ◯

Were its legs red? ◯

Male and female collared doves look identical, and they share in the care of their young. Juveniles lack the black collar.

My observations

_____
_____
_____
_____
_____
_____
_____
_____
_____
_____
_____
_____
_____

my drawings and photos

Collared dove
(*Streptopelia decaocto*)

The collared dove has become common in Britain only in the last 50 years, having migrated from India via Europe. This bird stays close to human society, and benefits in several ways. It feeds alongside farm poultry and cattle, sharing in their meals, and also hangs around sites such as docks, breweries, stables and zoos where there is grain to be found. It is seen in both towns and villages, and soon finds the local bird tables, turning up regularly for seeds and scraps. Where food is plentiful, the collared dove may feed in sizable flocks, especially in winter. It eats snails and insects as well as seeds.

SIZE
Length 28–32 cm, Weight 200 g

COLOUR
MALE Pale fawn-grey all over. Pinker tinge to underparts. Black half-collar at back of neck. Dark grey wing tips. Black bar under tail and white tip.
FEMALE Same as male.
WINTER DIFFERENCES None.

NEST
Loose platform of sticks, grass, roots. On buildings, in trees (preferably conifers), sometimes on ground.

CALL
Deep 'coo-coooo, coo'. 'Hwee' in flight.

RESIDENT/VISITOR
Resident.

narrow black half-collar

fawn-grey wings

♂♀

pinkish breast

QUICK ID
- Narrow black half-collar
- Black base under tail in flight
- All-over pale colouring
- Slimmer than pigeons

BEST TIME TO SPOT

	JAN	FEB	MAR	APR	MAY	JUN	JUL	AUG	SEP	OCT	NOV	DEC

6
5
4
3
2
1
0

Did you see it dive? ◯

Was it flying after another bird? ◯

Were there two birds flying together? ◯

Did it have yellow feet? ◯

When flying, a peregrine looks dark against the sky, but the outline of its wings and tail, and its white underparts help to identify it.

My observations

_____
_____
_____
_____
_____
_____
_____
_____
_____
_____
_____
_____
_____

my drawings and photos

Peregrine falcon
(Falco peregrinus)

In the past, peregrine falcons struggled to survive in Britain because they were hunted, and because of the effects of eating animals that had been poisoned by pesticides. In recent years, these beautiful birds of prey have enjoyed more protection, and their numbers are growing. Peregrines are famous for their swift, agile flight, and are the fastest animals in the world, especially when they swoop and dive to catch the birds they hunt. Males and females often fly in pairs, and the females are considerably bigger than their partners.

SIZE

Length 42 cm,
Weight 670–1100 g

COLOUR

MALE Blue-grey plumage on back. Darker head, white breast and pale underside with black bars.
FEMALE Same as the male.
WINTER DIFFERENCES None.

NEST

No nest. Eggs are laid in high places, such as cliff edges, tall buildings. Sometimes in the old nests of rooks or crows.

CALL

Loud calls of 'haak, haak, haak' and shrieks of 'kee-keeee'.

RESIDENT/VISITOR

Resident and visitor.

yellow eye ring

sharp, hooked bill

grey or black bars on underparts

♂ ♀

clawed talons

QUICK ID
- Short tail
- White breast with bars
- Small, rounded head
- Broad, pointed wings

BEST TIME TO SPOT

6
5
4
3
2
1
0

JAN FEB MAR APR MAY JUN JUL AUG SEP OCT NOV DEC

Did it have a long, four-barred tail? ◯

Was it alone? ◯

Did it have a distinctive 'kek-kek-kek' call? ◯

Was its throat white? ◯

This bird's long, broad wings and its unusually long tail help it to manoeuvre with great speed and agility when hunting.

My observations

_____
_____
_____
_____
_____
_____
_____
_____
_____
_____
_____

my drawings and photos

Sparrowhawk
(Accipiter nisus)

Sparrowhawks are becoming more common in large gardens, which is unfortunate for most visitors to the bird table, as the sparrowhawk specializes in catching small birds on the wing. When hunting, this smallish predator flies low over bushes and hedges, flapping and gliding, and weaves between tree trunks, catching its prey by surprise. The female, as in many birds of prey, is considerably larger than the male, and twice his weight. Once severely reduced in numbers due to the use of agricultural pesticides, the sparrowhawk now appears to be making a comeback.

SIZE
Length 28–38 cm,
Weight 130–320 g

COLOUR
MALE Dark grey back. White underparts, with close-spaced brown, horizontal bars.
FEMALE Duller and browner than male, also bigger.
WINTER DIFFERENCES None.

NEST
Made with sticks. In a tree, usually a conifer. Sometimes on a rocky ledge.

CALL
'Kek-kek-kek'.

RESIDENT/VISITOR
Resident.

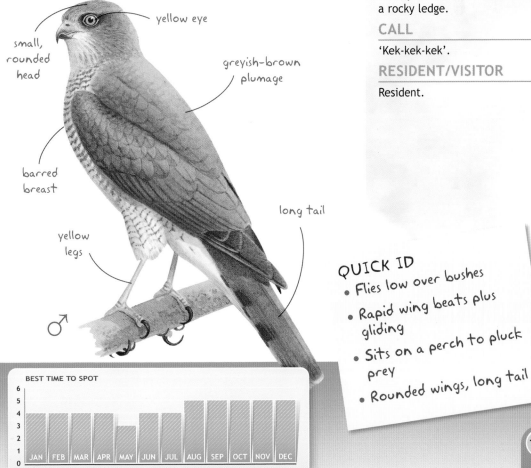

yellow eye

small, rounded head

greyish-brown plumage

barred breast

long tail

yellow legs

♂

QUICK ID
- Flies low over bushes
- Rapid wing beats plus gliding
- Sits on a perch to pluck prey
- Rounded wings, long tail

BEST TIME TO SPOT

6												
5												
4												
3												
2												
1												
0	JAN	FEB	MAR	APR	MAY	JUN	JUL	AUG	SEP	OCT	NOV	DEC

Did it look rather like a rook? ◯

Was it completely black all over? ◯

Did it have a short, heavy black bill? ◯

Did it make a loud 'kaaw' sound? ◯

Carrion crows are intelligent birds that are able to find prey in a variety of habitats. Their powerful bills can crack open shells.

My observations

_____
_____
_____
_____
_____
_____
_____
_____
_____
_____
_____
_____

my drawings and photos

Carrion crow
(Corvus corone)

The carrion crow feeds on dead animals (carrion means dead flesh), but will also kill small creatures such as mice and voles. It also steals both eggs and nestlings from small birds' nests. It is at home in the town as well as the countryside, and builds its nest in parks, squares and large gardens with mature trees. The carrion crow's powerful, curved beak is designed for tearing flesh, and sheep farmers claim that it attacks lambs or trapped sheep. On the coast it is known for cracking open crabs and shellfish by dropping them from a height onto rocks and roads.

SIZE
Length 47 cm, Weight 550 g

COLOUR
MALE Glossy black all over, with a black bill.
FEMALE Same as male.
WINTER DIFFERENCES None.

NEST
Made with twigs. High in a tree fork, or on a cliff ledge. In bushes in hill country.

CALL
Deep, drawn-out 'kaaw'.

RESIDENT/VISITOR
Resident. Some carrion crows come as winter visitors from Europe.

all over black plumage with blue sheen

short, heavy bill with small feathers at the base

strong perching toes with sharp claws

♂ ♀

QUICK ID
- All-black colouring including beak
- Much smaller than raven
- Neat, smooth plumage
- Nests singly, not in colonies

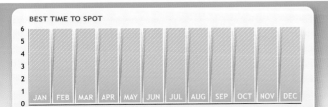

BEST TIME TO SPOT

	JAN	FEB	MAR	APR	MAY	JUN	JUL	AUG	SEP	OCT	NOV	DEC
6												
5												
4												
3												
2												
1												
0												

Did it look like a
smaller crow or rook? ○

Was the nape of its neck grey? ○

Did it have pale eyes? ○

Were its legs black? ○

Jackdaws can be distinguished from other crows by their dark faces surrounded by slate grey nape and cheeks.

My observations

_____

_____

_____

_____

_____

_____

_____

_____

_____

_____

_____

_____

my drawings and photos

Jackdaw
(Corvus monedula)

The jackdaw is a sociable bird, nesting in colonies in a variety of sites, including church towers, cliffs, ancient ruins and woodland trees. It also feeds in flocks in open countryside, moving rapidly over the ground looking for insects, caterpillars, worms and snails. The jackdaw happily invades the bird table, and will eat practically anything on offer, including seeds, scraps and cheese. Quicker and more agile than most members of the crow family, it can often be seen in mixed feeding flocks, which include rooks and starlings. During its mating rituals, the jackdaw raises its crown feathers and displays its silver-grey hood.

SIZE

Length 33 cm, Weight 220–270 g

COLOUR

MALE Black with a blue gloss. Ash-grey neck, nape and back of head. Black crown.
FEMALE Same as male.
WINTER DIFFERENCES None.

NEST

Twigs, with grass, wool and hair lining. In trees, rocky crevices, buildings, old nests, burrows. In colonies.

CALL

'Chuck-chuck' and 'chiup' danger call.

RESIDENT/VISITOR

Resident. Some birds move west in winter, as far as Ireland in some cases. There are also winter visitors from Europe.

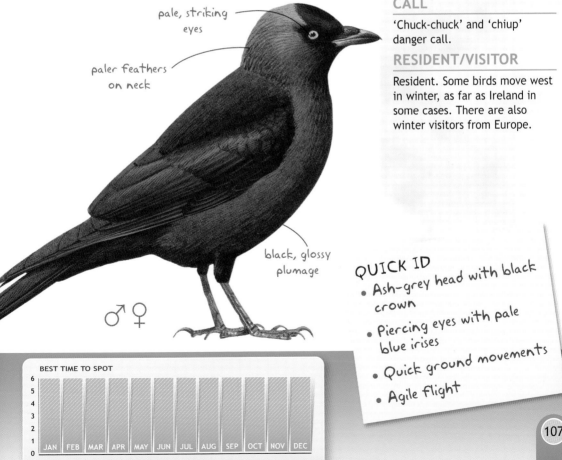

pale, striking eyes

paler feathers on neck

black, glossy plumage

♂ ♀

QUICK ID
- Ash-grey head with black crown
- Piercing eyes with pale blue irises
- Quick ground movements
- Agile flight

BEST TIME TO SPOT

JAN	FEB	MAR	APR	MAY	JUN	JUL	AUG	SEP	OCT	NOV	DEC

6
5
4
3
2
1
0

Was it mainly black and white? ◯

Did it have a long greenish-black tail? ◯

Were its wings blue-black? ◯

Was its bill long and thick? ◯

Despite their size, magpies are agile fliers that can swoop and dive from high perches into tight spots in pursuit of food.

My observations

my drawings and photos

Magpie
(Pica pica)

The subject of many country superstitions, the magpie is unmistakable with its contrasting plumage, long tail and loud voice. It is seen in town and country, and eats everything from berries, fruit, nuts, peas and grain to large table scraps and baby birds. Magpies are usually seen in pairs or small groups. It is often unwelcome in gardens with nest boxes, but is, in fact, far less of a problem for fledglings than the domestic cat. It is unpopular with gamekeepers who wage war on it for taking pheasant eggs. Like other crows, the magpie buries surplus food to eat later. It is also attracted to shiny objects, which it will also bury.

SIZE
Length 40–46 cm,
Weight 200–250 g

COLOUR
MALE White shoulders, flanks and belly. Black head, bill, upper breast and cape. Greenish shiny tail feathers with purple tips. Glossy blue-black wings.
FEMALE Same as male.
WINTER DIFFERENCES None.

NEST
Large domed structure of twigs. Roots and earth lining. In trees and hedgerows.

CALL
Harsh 'chak-ak-ak-a'.

RESIDENT/VISITOR
Resident.

blue-black wings

long greenish-black tail with rounded tip

white feathers underneath

♂ ♀

QUICK ID
- Contrasting black-and-white plumage
- Very long, graduated tail
- Loud, repeated call
- Noisy groups in winter

BEST TIME TO SPOT

	JAN	FEB	MAR	APR	MAY	JUN	JUL	AUG	SEP	OCT	NOV	DEC

Did it have blue-and-white patches on its wings? ◯

Did it have a black-and-white streaked head? ◯

Was its breast pinkish brown? ◯

Did it have a black moustache? ◯

Acorns are a favourite food of jays, although they sometimes forget where they have hidden them. Buried acorns may grow into oak trees.

My observations

my drawings and photos

Jay
(*Garrulus glandarius*)

The jay, despite its colourful plumage, is a member of the crow family. It is a shy bird. However, it has become bolder as it moves into suburban areas. It will come to the bird table, usually early in the morning, before humans are about. It is fond of peanuts, and shakes them to the ground from their suspended nets. The jay likes acorns, and sometimes hides them and beech mast in the ground. In the countryside, as well as eating wild foods, the jay consumes cultivated crops such as peas and corn. It also eats animal prey, including mice, small birds and their eggs, and insects.

SIZE
Length 34 cm, Weight 140–190 g

COLOUR
MALE Pinkish brown body. White rump. Black tail. White wing patches. Blue-and-black wing bars. Black-and-white crown feathers. Black moustache.
FEMALE Same as male.
WINTER DIFFERENCES None.

NEST
Twigs and earth, lined with roots and hair. Low in a tree.

CALL
Harsh 'skraak'.

RESIDENT/VISITOR
Resident.

streaked crown

pinkish brown body

blue feathers on wing

white flash on rump

black moustache

pink legs

♂ ♀

QUICK ID
- Pinkish body, blue wing bars
- Loud, harsh call
- White rump and black tail in flight
- Black and white crown feathers, sometimes raised

BEST TIME TO SPOT

JAN	FEB	MAR	APR	MAY	JUN	JUL	AUG	SEP	OCT	NOV	DEC

Was it slimmer than a crow? ◯

Did it have a bare area above its bill? ◯

Was it black all over? ◯

Did it have a cawing 'kaah' call? ◯

Flocks of rooks may swoop onto fields, especially when a field has been recently ploughed or a crop has been harvested.

My observations

_____
_____
_____
_____
_____
_____
_____
_____
_____
_____
_____
_____
_____
_____
_____

my drawings and photos

Rook
(Corvus frugilegus)

Rookeries, high in the tops of clumps of trees, are particularly noisy in spring, when the rooks quarrel over nest sites and go through their mating displays. The rook is the best-known British social bird, living in large colonies of nests, and travelling in flocks between the rookery and the feeding-grounds. The rook flies with a leisurely, slow, flapping and gliding flight. It feeds on pests such as caterpillars, snails, wire worms and beetle larvae, as well as grain from farmland. Occasionally it is attracted to garden bird tables when bones and fat are put out.

SIZE
Length 46 cm, Weight 480 g

COLOUR
MALE Glossy black plumage with a blue-green tint. Whitish featherless skin at the base of the bill.
FEMALE Same as male.
WINTER DIFFERENCES None.

NEST
Made with twigs and earth, lined with grass, moss, dead leaves. In treetops in a colony.

CALL
Deep 'kaah'.

RESIDENT/VISITOR
Resident. Some European migrants overwinter in Britain.

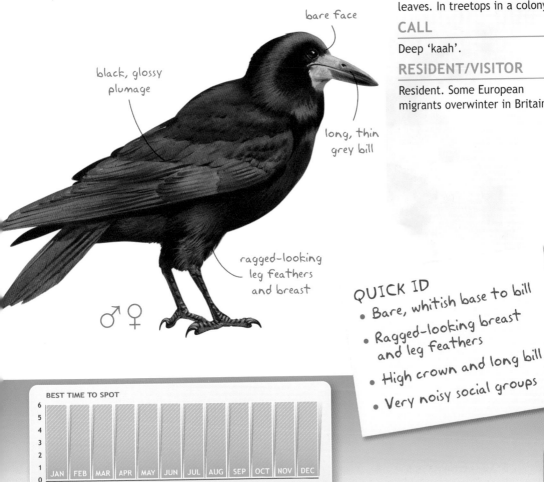

bare face

black, glossy plumage

long, thin grey bill

ragged-looking leg feathers and breast

♂ ♀

QUICK ID
- Bare, whitish base to bill
- Ragged-looking breast and leg feathers
- High crown and long bill
- Very noisy social groups

BEST TIME TO SPOT

	JAN	FEB	MAR	APR	MAY	JUN	JUL	AUG	SEP	OCT	NOV	DEC

Did it have a long, white neck? ◯

Did it have a black crest? ◯

Were its back and wings grey? ◯

Did it have long, yellow legs? ◯

Herons stand still in water, patiently waiting for prey. They strike suddenly and swiftly, then take the food to feed their young.

My observations

_____
_____
_____
_____
_____
_____
_____
_____
_____
_____
_____
_____
_____
_____

my drawings and photos

Grey heron
(Ardea cinerea)

The stately grey heron is found all over the British Isles, and is a familiar sight standing patiently in marshes and the shallows of lakes and rivers. It either stalks its prey with very slow movements, or waits motionless in order to surprise it with a sudden strike of its powerful, pointed bill. Prey is usually fish, but the heron also catches frogs, worms, insects and small mammals. Usually the only time it appears in the garden is when it drops in to eat the resident goldfish in the garden pond. The grey heron nests in colonies in the canopies of tall trees.

SIZE
Length 90–98 cm,
Weight 1.1–1.7 kg

COLOUR
MALE Grey wings and back. White neck and head. Black eye stripe and neck markings. Long black feathers protruding from back of head. Black tips and trailing edges to wings. Long yellow bill.
FEMALE Same as male.
WINTER DIFFERENCES None.

NEST
Large, built of sticks in tree-top colony.

CALL
'Kraak', and 'krreik' in flight.

RESIDENT/VISITOR
Resident.

black crest

long, pointed bill

white neck with black stripe

yellow legs

♂ ♀

QUICK ID
- Very lank, long-legged shape
- S-shaped kinked neck in flight
- Heavy, pointed yellow bill
- Stands in shallows fishing

BEST TIME TO SPOT

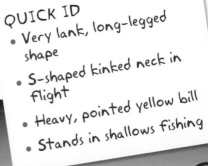

	6	5	4	3	2	1	0
JAN	FEB	MAR	APR	MAY	JUN	JUL	AUG	SEP	OCT	NOV	DEC

Did the bird have a red face? ◯

Was the tail long, barred black, pointed and brown? ◯

Was its crown green? ◯

Did it fly quite low? ◯

Wattles are usually seen in male birds, not females. A large colourful wattle shows that a male would make a good mate.

My observations

_____
_____
_____
_____
_____
_____
_____
_____
_____
_____
_____
_____
_____

my drawings and photos

Pheasant

(Phasianus colchicus)

Introduced centuries ago from Asia as a game bird, most pheasants are reared in controlled areas for shooting. However, many also live outside the artificial breeding pens. The pheasant has adapted well to the European woodlands. When alarmed it usually runs from danger, crouching low to the ground, but if approached too closely, erupts into the air with a startling clatter of wings before flying and gliding to safety. Due to unnaturally high numbers of birds bred for hunting, pheasants are frequent road casualties. A ground forager, the pheasant is often seen at the edge of woods, on farmland, and in parks and large gardens.

SIZE

Length 53–89 cm,
Weight 1–1.2 kg

COLOUR

MALE Red areas around eyes and side of face (wattles). Neck and crown dark metallic green. White neck ring. Ruddy brown plumage with horizontal lines of black 'scale' markings. Dark bars on tail.
FEMALE Light brown, with dark brown scale markings. No wattles.
WINTER DIFFERENCES None.

NEST

Hollow in the ground, lined with grass and leaves. Hidden in brambles, ferns, reeds, woodland undergrowth.

CALL

Loud 'kuk-kuk' plus whirr of wings when male proclaims territory. 'Tsik-tsik' by disturbed female. 'Gug-gug-gug' – taking off in alarm.

RESIDENT/VISITOR

Resident.

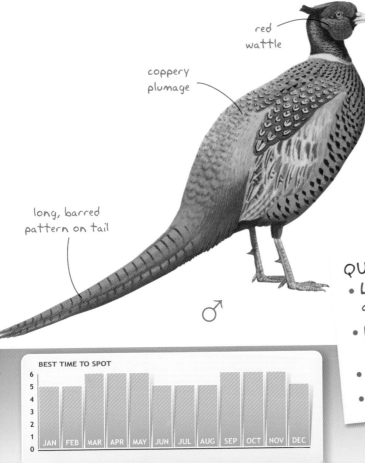

red wattle

coppery plumage

long, barred pattern on tail

♂

QUICK ID

- Loud territorial and alarm calls
- Red wattles and feather 'ears' of male
- Long tail, especially male
- Clattering take-off

BEST TIME TO SPOT

	JAN	FEB	MAR	APR	MAY	JUN	JUL	AUG	SEP	OCT	NOV	DEC

Was it near water? ◯

Did it have a waddling walk? ◯

Did you see any ducklings nearby? ◯

Did you hear a female's 'quack, quack'? ◯

Mallard ducklings stay near their mother. She protects them from predators and male mallards, which might attack them.

My observations

_____
_____
_____
_____
_____
_____
_____
_____
_____
_____
_____

my drawings and photos

Mallard
(Anas platyrhynchos)

Mallards are a common sight at ponds in town parks, by lakes and along riverbanks or canals. Males have a bright distinctive plumage compared to the plainer females. It can take a week for a female to lay up to 12 eggs in her nest. During this time, males protect their mates. The eggs are covered with a layer of leaves to hide them from predators. When the ducklings hatch they must wait for their feathers to dry before their mother leads them to the water to feed on plants and insects.

SIZE
Length 58 cm,
Weight 980–1200 g

COLOUR
MALE Grey/fawn body with a dark green head and orange bill. Purple-brown on the breast.
FEMALE Mostly brown body with cream streaks. Brown or orange bill.
WINTER DIFFERENCES The male may look slightly duller during the autumn moult.

NEST
Large nests are built among thick vegetation, often near the water's edge. They are made from leaves, grass and down.

CALL
Males deeply 'quork, quork', females loudly 'quack, quack'.

RESIDENT/VISITOR
Resident and winter visitor.

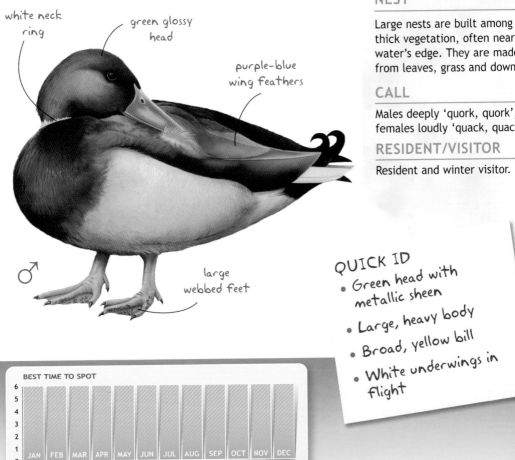

white neck ring

green glossy head

purple-blue wing feathers

♂

large webbed feet

QUICK ID
- Green head with metallic sheen
- Large, heavy body
- Broad, yellow bill
- White underwings in flight

BEST TIME TO SPOT

	JAN	FEB	MAR	APR	MAY	JUN	JUL	AUG	SEP	OCT	NOV	DEC

Was there a mound-like nest? ◯

Were cygnets with the adults? ◯

Was the bird aggressive? ◯

Were wings raised in a display posture? ◯

Mute swans fly with their long, slender necks extended, and with slow, deliberate and regular wingbeats.

My observations

my drawings and photos

Mute swan
(Cygnus olor)

Three types of swan can be spotted in the British Isles: Bewick's, whooper and mute. The mute is the most common and widespread, and it is the only type that can be seen in the summer. Mute swans have a distinctive black base to their orange bills, which is often slightly bigger in males (cobs) than females (pens). Mates for life, both parents take care of the grey-brown young (cygnets). These swans, especially the cobs, can be aggressive to people and other animals – spreading their wings and hissing to scare intruders away.

SIZE
Length 152 cm,
Weight 9–11.5 kg

COLOUR
MALE All white plumage. Reddish-orange bill with a black base.
FEMALE Same as male.
WINTER DIFFERENCES None.

NEST
Huge mound-shaped nests are built from dried grasses, sticks and other plants, usually near the water's edge.

CALL
Trumpets and hisses.

RESIDENT/VISITOR
Resident.

long, S-shaped neck

white plumage

large orange bill

♂ ♀

QUICK ID
- Very large body
- Orange bill with black base
- S-shaped neck
- All-white body

BEST TIME TO SPOT

	JAN	FEB	MAR	APR	MAY	JUN	JUL	AUG	SEP	OCT	NOV	DEC

Was it in a group? ◯

Did it have a black neck ring? ◯

Was it its plumage bright green? ◯

Did it have a very long tail? ◯

My observations

_____
_____
_____
_____
_____
_____
_____
_____
_____
_____
_____
_____
_____
_____

Parakeets are adept climbers because, like other parrots, their feet have two toes facing forwards and two facing backwards.

my drawings and photos

Ring-necked parakeet
(Psittacula krameri)

Few parrots can live in the cool climate of the British Isles, but Asian ring-necked parrots are an exception. They were originally kept as pets, but escapees have been able to breed successfully. Large flocks now thrive in southern areas, even in the winter. Also known as rose-necked parakeets, these colourful birds often visit gardens to eat fruit, berries and seeds, and take scraps from bird tables. They lay eggs from January to June, and both parents take care of the chicks.

SIZE

Length 41 cm, Weight 110–130 g

COLOUR

MALE Bright green plumage but the tail is slightly blue-green. Pink and black neck ring on males over three years old.
FEMALE The same as the male, but females lack the colourful neck ring. Tail is slightly shorter.
WINTER DIFFERENCES None.

NEST

Made from feathers and twigs. Usually in holes, such as old woodpecker holes or large nest boxes.

CALL

Loud squawking and squealing.

RESIDENT/VISITOR

Resident.

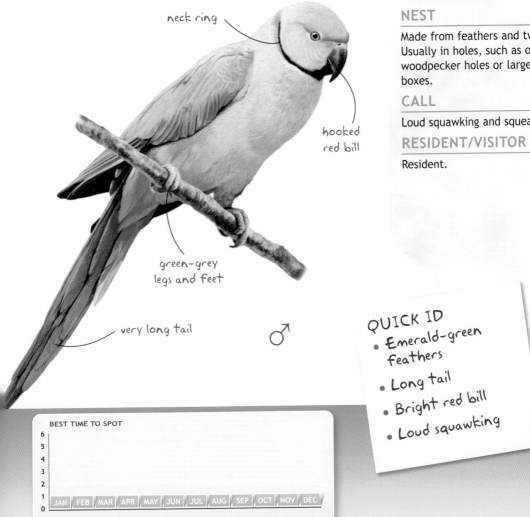

neck ring

hooked red bill

green-grey legs and feet

very long tail

♂

QUICK ID
- Emerald-green feathers
- Long tail
- Bright red bill
- Loud squawking

BEST TIME TO SPOT

6												
5												
4												
3												
2												
1												
0	JAN	FEB	MAR	APR	MAY	JUN	JUL	AUG	SEP	OCT	NOV	DEC

SEA AND COASTAL BIRDS

Was its crown black? ◯

Was its bill red? ◯

Did it have short red legs? ◯

Were its upperparts grey? ◯

Arctic terns breed in coastal areas, but they can be seen inland during the spring, when they are still migrating. Chicks fledge after 24 days.

My observations

_____

_____

_____

_____

_____

_____

_____

_____

_____

_____

_____

_____

_____

my drawings and photos

Arctic tern
(Sterna paradisaea)

The Arctic tern travels farther than any other bird. It breeds mainly in the Arctic, and winters at sea in the Antarctic. When migrating, it flies close to the sea surface, sometimes resting on floating objects. It breeds on rocky offshore islands, and can be seen nesting in large and small colonies around Scottish and Irish coasts, particularly in Shetland and Orkney. The Arctic tern fearlessly attacks intruders at its nest sites, and birdwatchers have even needed medical treatment after a mass attack. Sometimes known as the sea swallow, this graceful bird returns to the same nest each year.

SIZE
Length 32–35 cm,
Weight 80–110 g

COLOUR
MALE Pearl-grey upper plumage. White on rump and tail. White cheeks. Black cap. Blood-red bill in summer.
FEMALE Same as male.
WINTER DIFFERENCES Bill changes to pure black.

NEST
Simple hollow on ground, on rocks or shingle, sometimes grass-lined.

CALL
'Kee-arrr' and 'kee-kee'.

RESIDENT/VISITOR
Summer visitor, breeding in extreme north of Scotland.

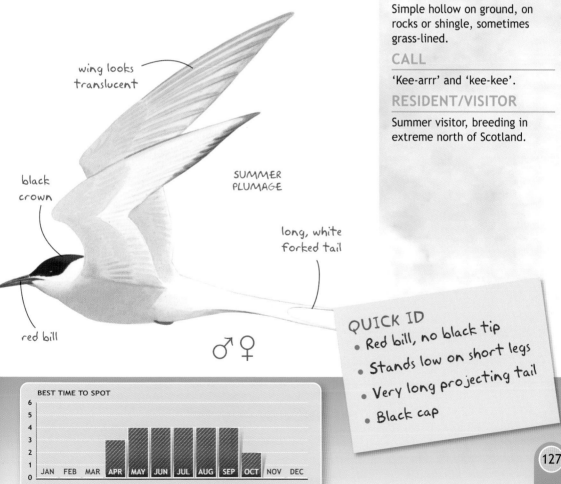

wing looks translucent

black crown

SUMMER PLUMAGE

long, white forked tail

red bill

♂ ♀

QUICK ID
- Red bill, no black tip
- Stands low on short legs
- Very long projecting tail
- Black cap

BEST TIME TO SPOT

	JAN	FEB	MAR	APR	MAY	JUN	JUL	AUG	SEP	OCT	NOV	DEC

Was its bill long and thin? ◯

Did its bill have a black tip? ◯

Were its upperparts grey? ◯

Did it have a black crown? ◯

Nests are built on the ground, so common tern chicks are dull brown to blend in with their surroundings.

My observations

_____

_____

_____

_____

_____

_____

_____

_____

_____

_____

_____

_____

_____

my drawings and photos

Common tern
(Sterna hirundo)

The common tern is often seen over rivers, hovering and swooping as it feeds. Elegant and aggressive, it is the most abundant tern found in Britain. It nests in noisy colonies, on beaches, sand dunes and islands. Colonies sometimes all take off at once, in silence, and fly over the sea before returning to their nest sites. A poor swimmer, the common tern also walks awkwardly on the ground because of its relatively short legs. In flight it is light and graceful, with rapid direction changes. It may live as long as ten years.

SIZE
Length 32–33 cm,
Weight 100–140 g

COLOUR
MALE Pale grey underparts and back. Dark grey band on wing undersides. Orange bill with black tip.
FEMALE Same as male.
WINTER DIFFERENCES Less black on crown. White marks on upperwing surfaces. Bill turns black with red base.

NEST
A hollow on the ground. Island sites popular. In colonies.

CALL
High-pitched 'KEE-yah', and 'kik-ik-ik-ik'.

RESIDENT/VISITOR
Visitor, arrives April and leaves October.

SUMMER PLUMAGE

♂ ♀

black crown

black tip to red bill

white undersides

translucent inner wing feathers

pale grey back

QUICK ID
- Dark band at back edge of wing undersides
- Red bill with black tip
- Paler undersides than Arctic tern
- Tail streamers no longer than closed wings

BEST TIME TO SPOT

| JAN | FEB | MAR | APR | MAY | JUN | JUL | AUG | SEP | OCT | NOV | DEC |

Did it have a white forehead? ◯

Was its bill yellow with a black tip? ◯

Were its legs yellow? ◯

Was it small and fast-flying? ◯

My observations

A male tern flies above a potential mate, displaying and calling to her. He then offers her a fish as a gift.

my drawings and photos

Little tern
(Sterna albifrons)

The little tern is tiny compared to other British terns. It nests on shingle ridges and sandy beaches, which brings it into conflict with holidaymakers. Like other terns it hovers and dives when fishing, and uses very fast wing beats, which give it a flickering flight. It can often be seen fishing right above the waves as they break on the beach. It dives for surface fish, but also catches insects on the wing. Its breeding colonies are small, and it flies around intruders repeating a 'duip' alarm call, then falling back until the coast is clear.

SIZE
Length 25 cm, Weight 50–60 g

COLOUR
MALE Pale grey back and wings. White rump and tail. Darker front edge to wings. Black cap and white forehead. Black stripe from eye. Yellow bill with black tip.
FEMALE Duller bill, feet and legs.
WINTER DIFFERENCES Crown mottled.

NEST
On ground in sand or shingle.

CALL
Fast 'kirri-ki-ki' and 'kyik'.

RESIDENT/VISITOR
Summer visitor, arriving April and leaving by September for West African coast.

white forehead

black stripe through eye

pale grey back

yellow bill with black tip

yellow-orange legs

♂♀

SUMMER PLUMAGE

black wing tips

QUICK ID
- Fast, flitting flight
- Very small black tip to bill
- Black eye stripe
- Short tail streamers

BEST TIME TO SPOT

JAN	FEB	MAR	APR	MAY	JUN	JUL	AUG	SEP	OCT	NOV	DEC

Was it quite a large bird? ◯

Was its black cap
ragged at the back? ◯

Were its legs black? ◯

Was its bill black with a yellow tip? ◯

From July, a sandwich tern begins to lose
its black cap. It grows white feathers on its
forehead and dark feathers on its outer wings.

My observations

_____
_____
_____
_____
_____
_____
_____
_____
_____
_____
_____
_____
_____
_____

my drawings and photos

Sandwich tern
(Sterna sandvicensis)

This is the largest of the terns visiting the British Isles. It is the first to arrive in the spring, and many pairs breed on shingle beaches, in coastal dunes, and around some inland waters. The noise of a large colony can be heard a considerable distance away. The sandwich tern likes being in large groups, and often mixes with other terns. It dives from a greater height than most terns when fishing and disappears entirely under water. It is also less aggressive towards intruders. It still swoops down but does not strike. It lives on sand eels, fish and molluscs. Once the young have left the nest, they may be fed by any of the adults in the group.

SIZE
Length 36–38 cm,
Weight 210–250 g

COLOUR
MALE Pearl-grey back and wings. White, sometimes pinkish underparts. Long black bill with small yellow tip. Black forehead, crown and nape.
FEMALE Same as male.
WINTER DIFFERENCES Forehead white. Crown and nape speckled with grey.

NEST
Scraped hollow on ground. In colonies.

CALL
Loud 'kirrik' and 'kik'.

RESIDENT/VISITOR
Visitor, arrives late March, departs October.

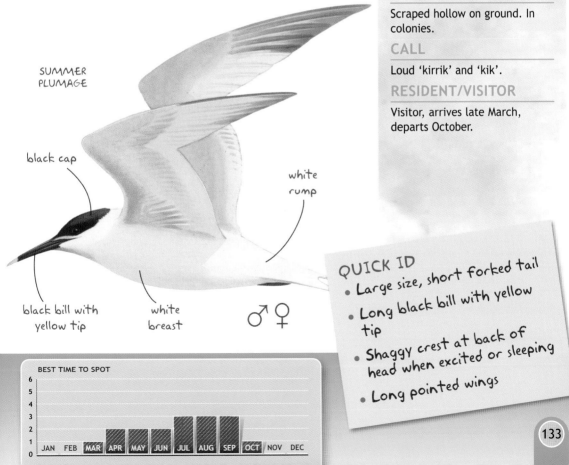

SUMMER PLUMAGE

black cap

white rump

black bill with yellow tip

white breast

♂ ♀

QUICK ID
- Large size, short forked tail
- Long black bill with yellow tip
- Shaggy crest at back of head when excited or sleeping
- Long pointed wings

BEST TIME TO SPOT

	JAN	FEB	MAR	APR	MAY	JUN	JUL	AUG	SEP	OCT	NOV	DEC

Was its flight gliding and soaring? ◯

If seen in summer, was its head dark brown? ◯

Was its outer underwing dark? ◯

Did it have a raucous call? ◯

In winter, the black-headed gull has a white head, dark 'ear' spot, vivid red legs and a bright red bill.

My observations

_____
_____
_____
_____
_____
_____
_____
_____
_____
_____
_____
_____
_____

my drawings and photos

Black-headed gull
(Chroicocephalus ridibundus)

One of the commonest British gulls, the black-headed gull is now found inland, both feeding and breeding, as often as on the shore. In its coastal habitat of low shores, harbours and estuaries, fish is an important part of its diet. However, its increased presence inland owes much to its enthusiasm for garbage dumps and the worms that surface from playing fields. Inland it feeds on insects, worms and snails as well as waste scraps and carrion. Black-headed gulls are often seen following a plough. They are fond of swimming, and outside the breeding season sometimes come into riverside cities.

SIZE
Length 35–38 cm,
Weight 230–260 g

COLOUR
MALE White neck, breast, underparts and back. Blue-grey wings. Chocolate-brown head in spring. Black wing tips. White leading edge to wings.
FEMALE Same as male.
WINTER DIFFERENCES White head, with dark 'ear' spot.

NEST
Grass and sticks. In marshes, sand-hills, lake islands, shingle. In colonies.

CALL
'Kwarr' and 'kwwup', plus a raucous scream. Long, squealing calls.

RESIDENT/VISITOR
Resident, but numbers swelled in winter by continental visitors.

chocolate-coloured head in summer

incomplete eye ring

dark red bill

SUMMER PLUMAGE

♂ ♀

black-tipped wings

long, red legs

QUICK ID
- Dark head in spring and summer
- Small size, slim shape
- Deep red bill and legs
- White leading edge to wings

BEST TIME TO SPOT

	JAN	FEB	MAR	APR	MAY	JUN	JUL	AUG	SEP	OCT	NOV	DEC

Was its bill yellowish in colour? ○

Were its wing tips black with white markings? ○

Was its breast white? ○

Was its back grey? ○

It will take three years for this chick to become an adult. During that time its plumage will slowly turn to white and grey.

My observations

my drawings and photos

Common gull

(*Larus canus*)

Far less common in England and Wales than its name suggests, the common gull is more numerous in Scotland, particularly in the north and the islands. A good swimmer and diver, it will submerge entirely in pursuit of fish. It is increasingly seen inland, usually in farming areas, and also around reservoirs and lakes. This scavenger will eat most things, including bird eggs. Common gulls are social birds, and they will gang up on a predator such as a hawk or a skua that is threatening the community.

SIZE

Length 40–42 cm,
Weight 350–450 g

COLOUR

MALE Pale grey upperparts. White underparts. Black-and-white patches at wing tips. Green-yellow bill and yellowy legs.
FEMALE Same as male.
WINTER DIFFERENCES Grey-brown streaks on head and breast.

NEST

Bulky, made of grass, seaweed, heather and moss. On ground or ledge.

CALL

High, shrill, squealing yelps and chattering cries.

RESIDENT/VISITOR

Resident in the north, but a winter visitor in the south.

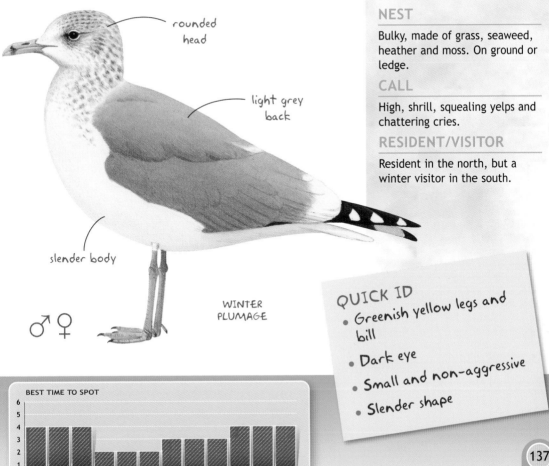

rounded head

light grey back

slender body

♂ ♀

WINTER PLUMAGE

QUICK ID
- Greenish yellow legs and bill
- Dark eye
- Small and non-aggressive
- Slender shape

BEST TIME TO SPOT

	JAN	FEB	MAR	APR	MAY	JUN	JUL	AUG	SEP	OCT	NOV	DEC

Was it a large bird? ◯

Did it have a red spot on its thick, yellow bill? ◯

Were its legs pale pink? ◯

Was its back black? ◯

Immature birds may appear large and powerful when in flight but they still lack the adult plumage, appearing brown and mottled.

My observations

_____

my drawings and photos

Great black-backed gull
(Larus marinus)

The great black-backed gull is an imposing bird, dramatically coloured, bulky and equipped with a powerful beak. It usually lives around rocky coasts and cliffs, although it is increasingly found in estuaries, and inland at reservoirs, tips and fields. A fearsome predator, it will also scavenge food. It can gulp down a whole rabbit, and will attack flocks of water birds in search of a meal. In winter it can often be seen around docks and fishing boats. The great black-backed gull can soar to great heights, and also skims the waves, like an albatross. It feeds on carrion when it gets the chance, and one of its local names is corpse-eater.

SIZE
Length 62–65 cm,
Weight 1.5–2 kg

COLOUR
MALE Black back and wings. White head and body. White wing tip spots. Yellow bill with red spot.
FEMALE Same colouring, but smaller, with smaller head and bill.
WINTER DIFFERENCES Faint streaks on head.

NEST
Large, made of heather, sticks, lined with grass or seaweed. In a clifftop hollow. Occasionally on moors.

CALL
Deep-pitched 'owk-uk-uk-uk'. Also wails and squeals.

RESIDENT/VISITOR
Resident, with many over-wintering visitors.

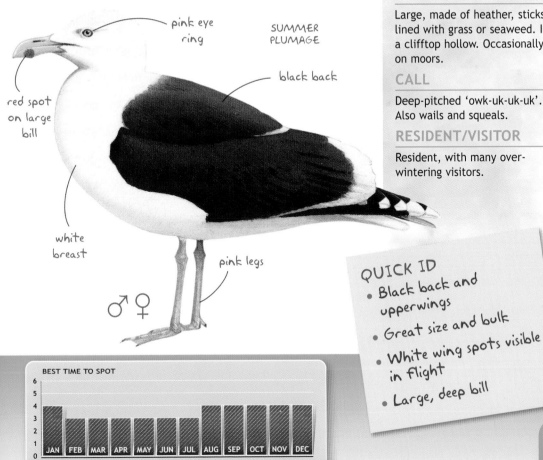

pink eye ring

SUMMER PLUMAGE

black back

red spot on large bill

white breast

pink legs

♂♀

QUICK ID
- Black back and upperwings
- Great size and bulk
- White wing spots visible in flight
- Large, deep bill

BEST TIME TO SPOT

| 6 | 5 | 4 | 3 | 2 | 1 | 0 |

JAN FEB MAR APR MAY JUN JUL AUG SEP OCT NOV DEC

Were its grey wings tipped with black? ◯

Was its flight strong and powerful? ◯

Did you see it near the land? ◯

Was its call loud? ◯

Herring gulls grab fish from the sea and can even plunge dive, although they remain near the surface of the water.

My observations

_____
_____
_____
_____
_____
_____
_____
_____
_____
_____
_____
_____
_____
_____

my drawings and photos

Herring gull

(Larus argentatus)

The most widespread of our coastal gulls, the herring gull is well known to holidaymakers at seaside towns and beaches, and has even taken to nesting on rooftops in resorts. It swiftly becomes tame, especially if fed, and has developed many feeding strategies such as trampling the ground to make worms come to the surface, and dropping crabs and shellfish onto rocks or tarmac to break them open. The herring gull is very skilful in flight, and follows fishing boats, gliding and riding the wind as it waits for fish scraps to be thrown overboard. In the winter it can sometimes be seen resting in flocks on fields and reservoirs.

SIZE
Length 52–55 cm,
Weight 750–1200 g

COLOUR
MALE Pale grey back. White head, neck and underparts. Black-and-white wing tips. Yellow bill with red spot.
FEMALE Same as male.
WINTER DIFFERENCES Dark streaks on head and breast. All plumage dirty white.

NEST
Untidy structure of available materials, including heather, seaweed and grasses.

CALL
'Kyow' repeated, and 'ga-ga-ga' when anxious.

RESIDENT/VISITOR
Resident, with many autumn/winter visitors from Europe.

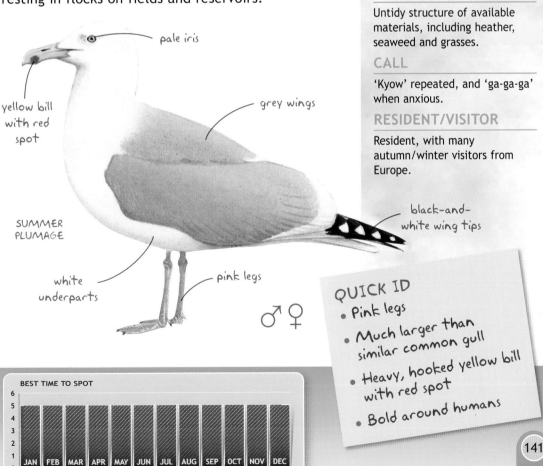

pale iris

grey wings

yellow bill with red spot

black-and-white wing tips

SUMMER PLUMAGE

white underparts

pink legs

♂ ♀

QUICK ID
- Pink legs
- Much larger than similar common gull
- Heavy, hooked yellow bill with red spot
- Bold around humans

BEST TIME TO SPOT

| JAN | FEB | MAR | APR | MAY | JUN | JUL | AUG | SEP | OCT | NOV | DEC |

Was its crown white? ◯

Was its back dark grey? ◯

Were its legs yellow? ◯

Was its bill yellow with a red spot? ◯

Females lay just one brood per year, in a simple ground nest. There are rarely more than three eggs in a brood.

My observations
_____
_____
_____
_____
_____
_____
_____
_____
_____
_____
_____
_____
_____

my drawings and photos

Lesser black-backed gull

(Larus fuscus)

A bird of islands, moors and clifftops, the lesser black-backed gull is a fierce predator of other seabirds, as well as of their eggs and young. It follows fishing boats and other vessels far out to sea, much farther than most other birds, often for hours at a time. Harbours and dumps are favourite places for it to scavenge. Very protective of its nest and young, a whole colony will take to the air to drive off intruders. Chicks leave the nest a few days after hatching, and forage on the ground, guarded by their parents for at least six weeks.

SIZE

Length 50–58 cm,
Weight 600–1000 g

COLOUR

MALE Slate-grey wing backs. Black wing tips with white spots.
FEMALE Same as male.
WINTER DIFFERENCES Grey-brown head and dull yellow legs.

NEST

On the ground, in colonies. Heather stalks and seaweed.

CALL

Loud, deep 'ow-ow-ow-kyow'.

RESIDENT/VISITOR

Summer breeding visitor, arriving in February, and leaving for Portugal and North Africa in November. Some birds over winter in Britain.

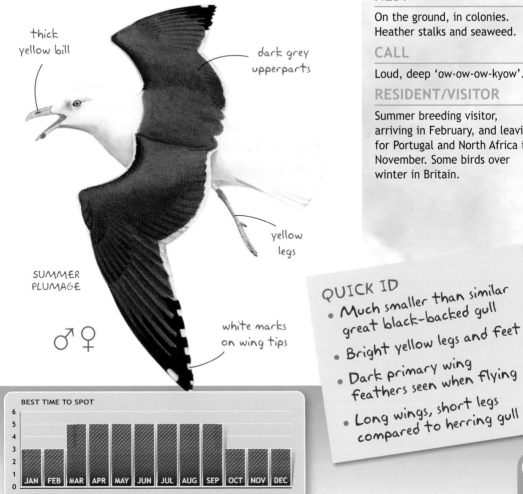

thick yellow bill

dark grey upperparts

yellow legs

SUMMER PLUMAGE

♂♀

white marks on wing tips

QUICK ID
- Much smaller than similar great black-backed gull
- Bright yellow legs and feet
- Dark primary wing feathers seen when flying
- Long wings, short legs compared to herring gull

BEST TIME TO SPOT

| JAN | FEB | MAR | APR | MAY | JUN | JUL | AUG | SEP | OCT | NOV | DEC |

Was its bill red and slightly drooping? ◯

If in summer, was its head black? ◯

Were its legs red? ◯

Were its back and wings pale grey? ◯

In the summer, an adult Mediterranean gull has a black head. The juvenile gull will soon begin to develop a grey plumage.

My observations

my drawings and photos

Mediterranean gull

(Larus melanocephalus)

Rare in Britain, but increasing in numbers, the Mediterranean gull can sometimes be found around eastern and southern coasts in marshes and coastal flat lands. Closely related to the British black-headed gull, the Mediterranean gull is a bulkier bird, with a heavier bill and longer legs. It feeds mainly on insects, crabs and small fish. It usually breeds in the Balkans and southeastern Europe, but about 110 pairs now breed annually in the British Isles, joined by around 1800 birds in winter. Small numbers may also be found around gatherings of black-headed and common gulls, such as near reservoirs

SIZE

Length 36–38 cm,
Weight 300–400 g

COLOUR

MALE Pearl-grey upperwings. White underwings. Black hood. Red bill.
FEMALE Same as male.
WINTER DIFFERENCES Black hood becomes mottled. Bill is darker. Dark smudge around and behind eye.

NEST

On the ground near water, in colonies. Rare in Britain.

CALL

'Keeow' and 'ayeeah'. When alarmed 'ga-ga-ga'.

RESIDENT/VISITOR

Mainly a spring visitor, though some pairs spend the winter and nest.

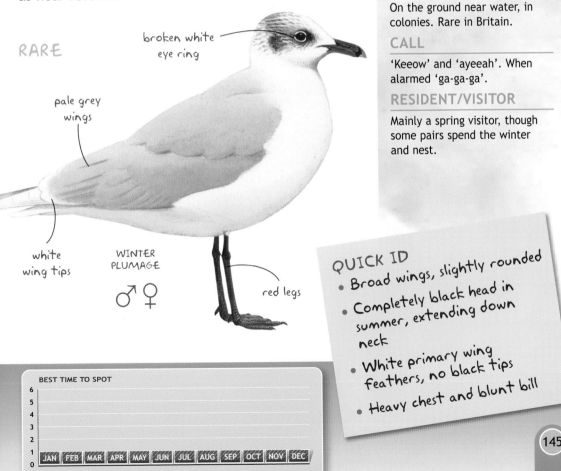

RARE

broken white eye ring

pale grey wings

white wing tips

WINTER PLUMAGE

♂ ♀

red legs

QUICK ID
- Broad wings, slightly rounded
- Completely black head in summer, extending down neck
- White primary wing feathers, no black tips
- Heavy chest and blunt bill

BEST TIME TO SPOT

| | JAN | FEB | MAR | APR | MAY | JUN | JUL | AUG | SEP | OCT | NOV | DEC |
6
5
4
3
2
1
0

Did it have a spiked tail? ◯

Was it flying low over the water? ◯

Was its belly white? ◯

Did it have a high voice? ◯

This is the darker form of the adult Arctic skua. Young birds have a slight reddish-brown tint to the dark plumage.

My observations

_____
_____
_____
_____
_____
_____
_____
_____
_____
_____
_____
_____
_____

my drawings and photos

Arctic skua
(*Stercorarius parasiticus*)

The fast and acrobatic Arctic skua relentlessly chases puffins, kittiwakes and terns to make them bring up fish they have eaten, which it then catches and eats in mid-air. During the chase it sprints and turns like a hawk. Its normal flight is steady and graceful. The Arctic skua's attacks on terns are particularly successful. When protecting its nest and young, it will attack anything from sheep to humans. The colony usually posts two or three sentry birds to give the alarm when predators or other intruders approach. As well as fish, the Arctic tern kills and eats adult and young birds, and will also feed on carrion.

SIZE
Length 41–46 cm,
Weight 350–550 g

COLOUR
MALE Two forms. Light form – blackish crown. Dark upperparts. White underparts. Dark breast band. Dark form – blackish brown all over, slightly paler underparts.
FEMALE Same as male.
WINTER DIFFERENCES Light form becomes barred above and below.

NEST
On the ground on moors, in colonies.

CALL
Wailing and a squealing 'eee-air'.

RESIDENT/VISITOR
Summer breeding visitor to northern Scotland and islands. Arrives late April, departs late October. Offshore migrant on most British coasts in autumn.

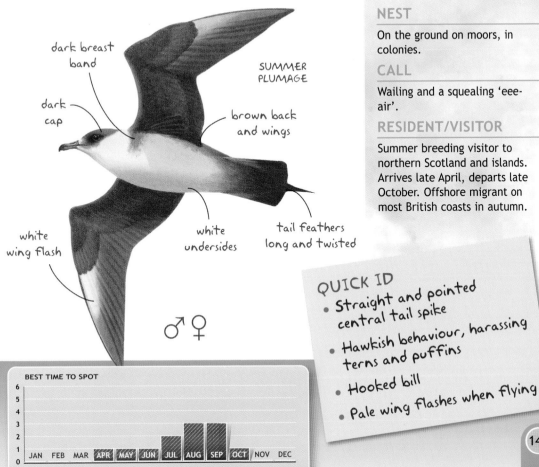

dark breast band

SUMMER PLUMAGE

dark cap

brown back and wings

white wing flash

white undersides

tail feathers long and twisted

♂ ♀

QUICK ID
- Straight and pointed central tail spike
- Hawkish behaviour, harassing terns and puffins
- Hooked bill
- Pale wing flashes when flying

BEST TIME TO SPOT

	JAN	FEB	MAR	APR	MAY	JUN	JUL	AUG	SEP	OCT	NOV	DEC

Did it look like a big brown gull? ◯

Were its legs brown? ◯

Did it have white wing patches? ◯

Did it have a bulky shape? ◯

With a wingspan of up to 140 cm, large clawed feet and hooked bill, a great skua can easily threaten a sheep.

My observations

my drawings and photos

Great skua

(Catharacta skua)

The bulky great skua chases birds to steal their meals as other skuas do, but goes for large prey, such as gannets, gulls and ducks. In the summer it also kills and eats other sea birds. It brings down its prey by dive-bombing it from a great height. Once almost extinct in the British Isles, the great skua has made a comeback, and is a regular summer resident in northern sites in the Orkney and Shetland islands. It is rarely seen inland in winter. It makes alarming attacks on intruders to its nest-sites, swooping down in a steep dive and striking with its feet as it sweeps past.

SIZE

Length 53–58 cm,
Weight 1300–2000 g

COLOUR

MALE Dark brown speckled plumage. Darker cap. Dark wings with conspicuous white underwing patches. Rusty brown underparts. Black legs and bill.
FEMALE Same as male.
WINTER DIFFERENCES None.

NEST

On ground near sea in colonies.

CALL

Harsh 'skeerr', also 'tuh-tuh' when attacking.

RESIDENT/VISITOR

Breeding visitor to northern islands in summer. Migrates south for West Africa, mid-Atlantic and South America in winter.

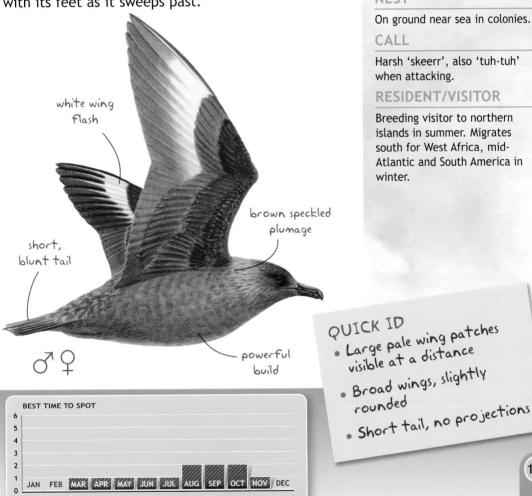

white wing flash

short, blunt tail

brown speckled plumage

powerful build

♂ ♀

QUICK ID
- Large pale wing patches visible at a distance
- Broad wings, slightly rounded
- Short tail, no projections

BEST TIME TO SPOT

6												
5												
4												
3												
2												
1												
0	JAN	FEB	MAR	APR	MAY	JUN	JUL	AUG	SEP	OCT	NOV	DEC

Was it a crow-like bird? ◯

Was it black all over? ◯

Were its bill and legs red? ◯

Were its wings finger-like at the tips? ◯

A chough scours the undergrowth for signs of prey. It uses its long bill to dig into the soil, reaching far down to find grubs.

My observations

_____
_____
_____
_____
_____
_____
_____
_____
_____
_____
_____
_____

my drawings and photos

Chough

(Pyrrhocorax pyrrhocorax)

The chough is the rarest member of the crow family in Britain, and is easily distinguished from other crows. It is found along coastal cliffs, swooping along and calling loudly, and often flies in small flocks. It is particularly acrobatic during the spring nesting season, soaring and tumbling, and even turning upside down. The chough feeds inland of the cliffs on the fields where it nests. It eats insects and worms, as well as dropping down to sea level to eat little crabs and shellfish. It sometimes feeds on grain left in stubble after harvesting. In 2002, wild chicks hatched in Cornwall, where the chough is the county's official bird, for the first time in 50 years.

SIZE
Length 40 cm, Weight 280–360 g

COLOUR
MALE Glossy blue-black all over. Red bill and legs.
FEMALE Same as male.
WINTER DIFFERENCES None.

NEST
Simple hollow on the ground, on rocks or shingle, sometimes grass-lined.

CALL
'Kweeow' or 'chee-ah'.

RESIDENT/VISITOR
Resident.

RARE

curved
red bill

square-shaped
tail

black
plumage

♂ ♀

QUICK ID
- Long, curved, red bill and red legs
- Coastal cliff habitat
- Distinctive call
- Aerobatic flight on very broad wings

BEST TIME TO SPOT

6												
5												
4												
3												
2												
1												
0	JAN	FEB	MAR	APR	MAY	JUN	JUL	AUG	SEP	OCT	NOV	DEC

Was it pale grey with shiny neck patches? ◯

Did its folded wing show two black bars? ◯

Was its bill black and white? ◯

Were its legs pink? ◯

Rock doves perch on cliff faces, but build their nests in more sheltered ledges and cavities. They breed all year round.

My observations

my drawings and photos

Rock dove

(Columba livia)

The rock dove is the ancestor of all domestic pigeons. These were originally bred from wild birds for eating and for racing. The feral pigeons seen in both town and country are descendants of domestic escapees. In its natural state the rock dove lives among the rocks and cliffs of coasts and islands. It feeds on seeds and plant material in fields and woods, and perches on rocks or on the ground in preference to trees. Very few pure rock doves survive due to interbreeding with feral relatives. Those that remain breed on cliffs in northwestern Scotland and western Ireland.

SIZE

Length 31–34 cm,
Weight 250–350 g

COLOUR

MALE Bluish body. Light grey back and wings. Double dark wing bars. Metallic green-and-purple neck. White rump and underwing.
FEMALE Same as male.
WINTER DIFFERENCES None.

NEST

Roots, seaweed, heather on rocky ledge.

CALL

'Ruh-ruh-ruh'.

RESIDENT/VISITOR

Resident.

RARE

double black wing bars

black-and-white bill

metallic-looking neck pattern

♂ ♀

QUICK ID
- White underwings and rump
- Double wing bars
- No black on wing tips
- Flies low over water

BEST TIME TO SPOT

JAN	FEB	MAR	APR	MAY	JUN	JUL	AUG	SEP	OCT	NOV	DEC

6
5
4
3
2
1
0

Were its upperparts dark chocolate brown in colour? ◯

Was its bill thin and pointed? ◯

Were its legs short and black? ◯

Was its breast white? ◯

My observations

During the summer breeding season, guillemot colonies nest on sheer cliffs. Females lay just one egg.

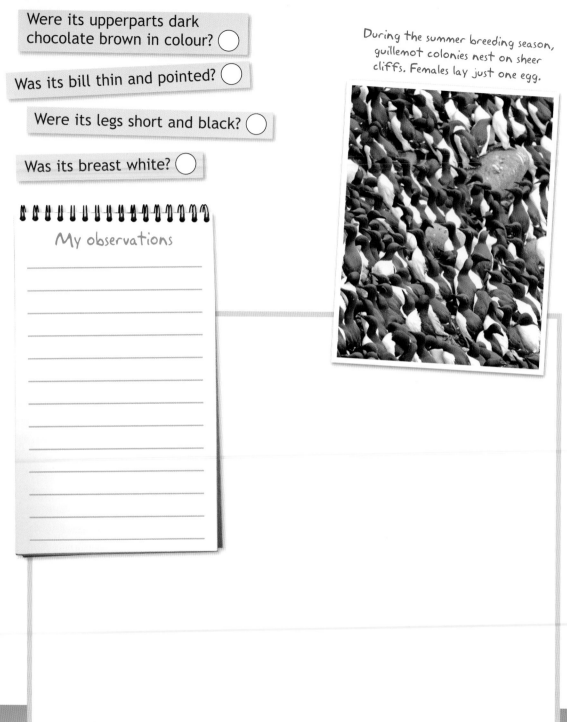

my drawings and photos

Guillemot
(Uria aalge)

The guillemot spends much of its life at sea, coming ashore to breed in packed colonies on cliff ledges and on the flat tops of off-shore rock stacks. Groups of guillemots fly up to 50 kilometres to their feeding-grounds each day. Their relatively short wings have a fast, whirring beat as they skim low over the water. The guillemot is a strong and expert swimmer, diving as deep as 50 metres in pursuit of fish. About three weeks after hatching, the guillemot chick leaps down from the cliffs to the water or rocks below, where it is joined by the male parent, which leads it out to sea.

SIZE

Length 38–54 cm,
Weight 750–1000 g

COLOUR

MALE Dark chocolate-brown head and upper body. White undersides with brown streaks on flanks. So-called 'bridled' birds have a narrow white eye ring extending into a line behind the eye.
FEMALE Same as male.
WINTER DIFFERENCES White chin, sides of head, neck. Dark line extends back from eye.

NEST

No nest is made. Eggs are laid on cliff ledges, in dense colonies. Sometimes among boulders.

CALL

Extended 'aarrgh'.

RESIDENT/VISITOR

Resident.

SUMMER PLUMAGE

pointed bill

blackish-brown plumage

white underparts

short, rounded tail

♂♀

QUICK ID
- Dagger-like bill
- Dark chocolate-brown tinge to plumage
- Dark brown streaks in flanks
- Smaller and slimmer than a razorbill

BEST TIME TO SPOT

JAN	FEB	MAR	APR	MAY	JUN	JUL	AUG	SEP	OCT	NOV	DEC

Did its wings have white patches? ◯

Was the rest of its plumage black? ◯

Was the inside of its mouth bright red? ◯

Were its legs short and red? ◯

Unlike most other members of the auk family in Europe, black guillemots are likely to be seen alone, or in pairs.

My observations

_____
_____
_____
_____
_____
_____
_____
_____
_____
_____
_____
_____
_____

my drawings and photos

Black guillemot
(Cepphus grylle)

The black guillemot is about the size of a pigeon, and nests in small groups, not gathering like the guillemot in huge colonies. It flies fast and low, and can swim expertly under water, catching small fish and seabed creatures such as worms and molluscs. It is found around the coasts of Ireland and north and west Scotland, in Anglesey in Wales, and Cumbria in England. When threatening intruders it opens its beak very wide to reveal the bright red interior. It tends to stay closer to land than other guillemots, fishing in shallow waters. It winters at sea, not too far from its breeding territories, returning each year to the same nest site.

SIZE
Length 30–32 cm,
Weight 340–450 g

COLOUR
MALE Black plumage all over, except for large white wing patches. Bright red feet.
FEMALE Same as male.
WINTER DIFFERENCES Whitish underparts and head, with pale barring. Wings barred deep grey and white. White wing patches remain.

NEST
No nest made. Among boulders, in crevices on rocky shores and cliffs.

CALL
Very high-pitched whistles and whines. 'Dinsie-dinsie'.

RESIDENT/VISITOR
Resident.

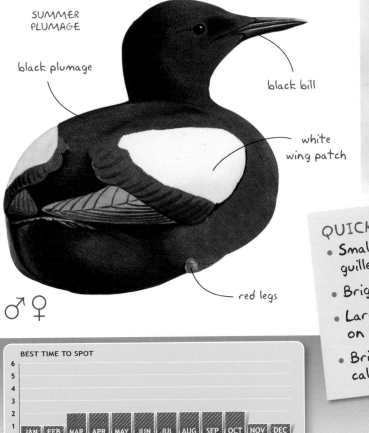

SUMMER PLUMAGE

black plumage

black bill

white wing patch

red legs

♂ ♀

QUICK ID
- Small size compared to a guillemot
- Bright red legs and feet
- Large white patches visible on both sides of wings
- Bright red gape when calling or threatening

BEST TIME TO SPOT

| | JAN | FEB | MAR | APR | MAY | JUN | JUL | AUG | SEP | OCT | NOV | DEC |
6
5
4
3
2
1
0

Did it have a short, stubby, yellow bill? ◯

Did it look gull-like? ◯

Were its legs yellow? ◯

Was it grey and white? ◯

When a fulmar is seen on land it will be sitting, not walking. These birds have very weak legs and are unable to stand.

My observations

_____
_____
_____
_____
_____
_____
_____
_____
_____
_____
_____
_____
_____
_____

my drawings and photos

Fulmar

(Fulmarus glacialis)

The fulmar is a true seabird that never feeds on land. It can glide like an albatross on stiff wings over a metre wide, staying close to the sea surface. It is found all around the British coast, wherever there are cliffs on which to nest. The fulmar spends most of its time at sea, and is an enthusiastic follower of fishing boats. A large increase in British fulmar numbers in the 20th century may have been due to plentiful supplies of fish waste and offal from trawlers and whalers. Fulmars defend their nests energetically, and may eject a foul-smelling 'fulmar oil' at persistent intruders.

SIZE
Length 45–50 cm,
Weight 750 g

COLOUR
MALE White head and underparts. Brownish-grey upperwings and body. Yellow legs.
FEMALE Same as male.
WINTER DIFFERENCES None.

NEST
On cliff ledges in colonies.

CALL
Cackling 'ag-ag-ag-arrr'.

RESIDENT/VISITOR
Resident.

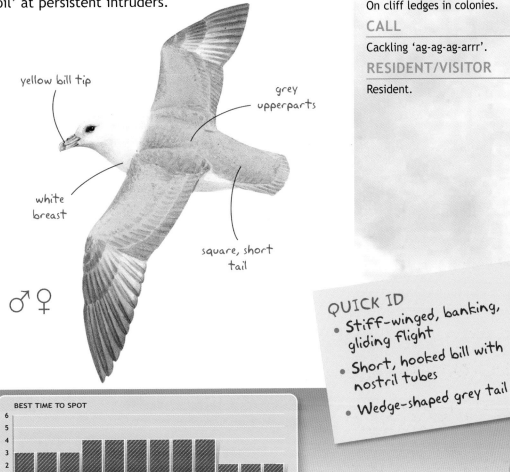

yellow bill tip

grey upperparts

white breast

square, short tail

♂♀

QUICK ID
- Stiff-winged, banking, gliding flight
- Short, hooked bill with nostril tubes
- Wedge-shaped grey tail

BEST TIME TO SPOT

| JAN | FEB | MAR | APR | MAY | JUN | JUL | AUG | SEP | OCT | NOV | DEC |

Did its call sound like
its name (kitti-way-ake)? ◯

Did it have black legs? ◯

Was it white-breasted
with grey wings? ◯

Did it have black wing tips? ◯

The kittiwake is only seen on land when it
is the breeding season, around May to June.
Females have one to three chicks.

My observations

_____
_____
_____
_____
_____
_____
_____
_____
_____
_____
_____
_____
_____

my drawings and photos

Kittiwake

(Rissa tridactyla)

The kittiwake usually fishes on the surface of the sea, and never scavenges the tideline like other gulls. It feeds on fish, crustaceans, worms and trawler waste. The kittiwake is the smallest of the gulls breeding in the British Isles. It spends the winter at sea, and the spring and summer on some of the most inaccessible and sheer cliff ledge nest sites in the country. In flight the kittiwake is graceful, and it moves faster than larger gulls, using rapid wing beats. It dives like a tern from the air when fishing, and uses its wings to swim underwater.

SIZE

Length 38–41 cm,
Weight 350–440 g

COLOUR

MALE Grey back. Black wing tips. White head and body. Greenish-yellow bill.
FEMALE Same as male.
WINTER DIFFERENCES
Nape and crown turn darker grey.

NEST

Seaweed, moss and grass, moulded with mud into a firm cup. On tiny ledges in crowded colonies.

CALL

'Kitti-way-ake'.

RESIDENT/VISITOR

Resident breeder, with a small number of winter visitors.

SUMMER PLUMAGE

black wing tips

grey back

dark eye

white underparts

♂ ♀

QUICK ID
- Distinctive 'kittiwake' call
- Black wing tips
- Slender greenish-yellow bill
- Black three-toed feet

BEST TIME TO SPOT

	JAN	FEB	MAR	APR	MAY	JUN	JUL	AUG	SEP	OCT	NOV	DEC

Did it have a parrot-like, colourful bill? 〇

Were its upperparts black? 〇

Did it have a white face? 〇

Were its legs short and red? 〇

Puffins spend about six months at sea and return to land to breed. They reinstate the bond with their mate by tapping bills together.

My observations

_____
_____
_____
_____
_____
_____
_____
_____
_____
_____
_____
_____
_____
_____
_____

my drawings and photos

Puffin
(Fratercula arctica)

The puffin is unmistakeable, with its black crown and colourful summer bill contrasting with its white face. It breeds in large colonies in Britain and Ireland. It is an accomplished diver and swimmer, frequently diving up to 15 metres, and is capable of catching several fish without surfacing. It holds them cross-wise in its large bill. Puffins choose the grassy slopes at the top of cliffs for their breeding-sites, and build their nests in burrows. They either excavate these themselves, or use old rabbit or shearwater burrows. Puffins have large, strong feet that they use as brakes when landing, as well as for swimming and digging burrows.

SIZE
Length 30 cm, Weight 400 g

COLOUR
MALE Black cap, neck and upperparts. White face. Bright red, yellow and blue bill. Red eye ring. Small blue markings above and below eye. Orangey-red feet.
FEMALE Same as male.
WINTER DIFFERENCES Dark grey face, bill smaller and duller.

NEST
At the end of a burrow, up to 2 m deep.

CALL
A growling 'ka-arr-arr' in the colony.

RESIDENT/VISITOR
Resident.

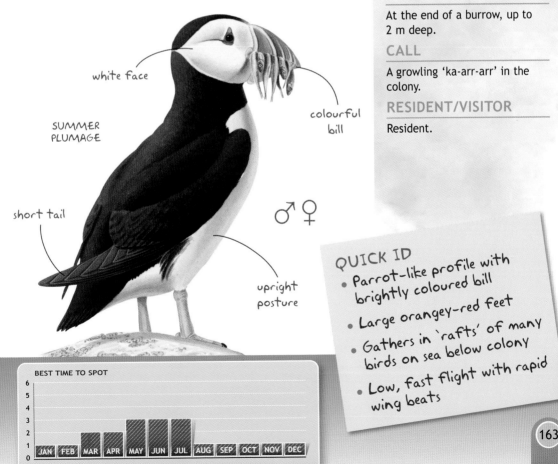

white face

SUMMER PLUMAGE

colourful bill

short tail

♂ ♀

upright posture

QUICK ID
- Parrot-like profile with brightly coloured bill
- Large orangey-red feet
- Gathers in 'rafts' of many birds on sea below colony
- Low, fast flight with rapid wing beats

BEST TIME TO SPOT

	JAN	FEB	MAR	APR	MAY	JUN	JUL	AUG	SEP	OCT	NOV	DEC

Was its bill black with a white vertical line? ◯

Were its upperparts black? ◯

Were its underparts white? ◯

Did it look like an auk? ◯

My observations

_____
_____
_____
_____
_____
_____
_____
_____
_____
_____
_____
_____
_____

An adult feeds fish to its chick. Razorbills have just one chick at a time. Although they look like penguins, they are not closely related.

my drawings and photos

Razorbill

(Alca torda)

There are more than 180,0000 breeding pairs of razorbills in Britain and Ireland. The razorbill is ungainly on land, and walks with a shuffle, but is perfectly at home in the sea, where it is an excellent swimmer. When feeding its young, it can carry up to a dozen small fish at a time in its large beak. Razorbills start to come ashore near their breeding site in February, but do not begin nesting and breeding until March or later. They begin to leave the site again in July. They spend the entire winter at sea, unless driven ashore by particularly strong storms. British breeding birds migrate as far as the Mediterranean in winter.

SIZE
Length 40 cm, Weight 700 g

COLOUR
MALE Black upper body, head, bill and wings. White underparts.
FEMALE Same as male.
WINTER DIFFERENCES Chin, throat, sides of neck turn white. White bill markings turn grey.

NEST
Rocky crevices, cliff ledges and among boulders. In colonies, often mixed with kittiwakes and guillemots.

CALL
A grating 'grrr' in the colony.

RESIDENT/VISITOR
Resident breeder, wintering at sea as far south as the Mediterranean.

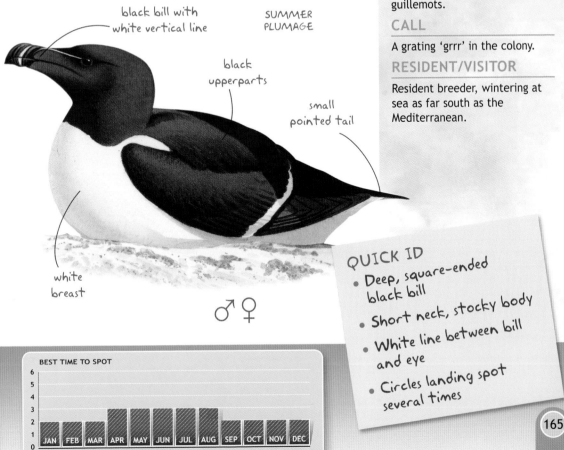

black bill with white vertical line

SUMMER PLUMAGE

black upperparts

small pointed tail

white breast

♂ ♀

QUICK ID
- Deep, square-ended black bill
- Short neck, stocky body
- White line between bill and eye
- Circles landing spot several times

BEST TIME TO SPOT

	JAN	FEB	MAR	APR	MAY	JUN	JUL	AUG	SEP	OCT	NOV	DEC

Was it flying low over the water? ◯

Was it black above? ◯

Did it have a white breast, belly and throat? ◯

Were its legs short and grey? ◯

As the weather cools and winter approaches, Manx shearwaters begin the long flight back to the waters off Brazil.

My observations

my drawings and photos

Manx shearwater
(Puffinus puffinus)

The Manx shearwater elegantly skims the waves, following the water contours, tipping first one way, then the other. It breeds mainly on islands off the Irish coast and the English west coast. It has a habit of congregating on the water below the breeding site at dusk, not coming ashore until after dark, possibly to avoid predators. With its effortless, gliding flight, the Manx shearwater can travel great distances to feed, sometimes as much as 300 kilometres. Its food includes fish, crustaceans and invertebrates all picked off the sea surface. These birds cannot walk well on land, spending most of their time at sea.

SIZE
Length 30–38 cm, Weight 440 g

COLOUR
MALE Black upperparts. White underparts. Black wing tips and trailing edges of wings.
FEMALE Same as male.
WINTER DIFFERENCES None.

NEST
In a burrow, up to 1.5 m long, excavated in soft earth. A small amount of dry grass bedding.

CALL
'Kookoo- kooroo'.

RESIDENT/VISITOR
A summer breeder, visiting Britain between February and October and wintering at sea.

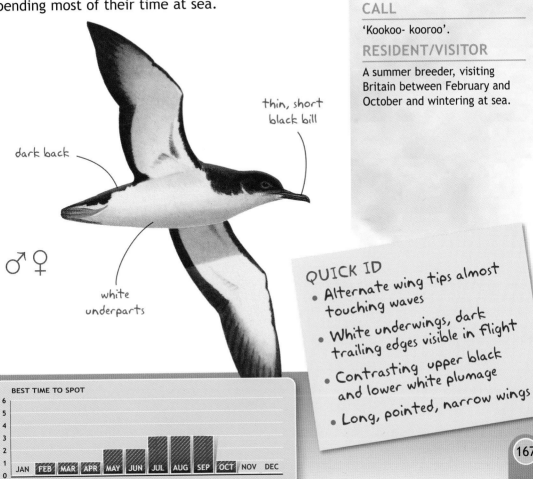

dark back

thin, short black bill

♂♀

white underparts

QUICK ID
- Alternate wing tips almost touching waves
- White underwings, dark trailing edges visible in flight
- Contrasting upper black and lower white plumage
- Long, pointed, narrow wings

BEST TIME TO SPOT

| | JAN | FEB | MAR | APR | MAY | JUN | JUL | AUG | SEP | OCT | NOV | DEC |

Did it look rather goose-like? ◯

Did it have short, black legs? ◯

Was its plumage glossy black? ◯

Did it have impressive open wings? ◯

Cormorants often return to the same nesting place year after year. They lay up to four eggs between April and May.

My observations

my drawings and photos

Cormorant

(Phalacrocorax carbo)

The cormorant is often seen drying its feathers, perched with wings outstretched. When it swims, its feathers become saturated, which aids the underwater pursuit of fish. When it catches a fish, a cormorant brings it to the surface and shakes it vigorously before swallowing it. Although birds of coasts, tidal rivers and large lakes, cormorants are often seen far inland, flying with powerful, steady wing beats. As well as for swimming, the large webbed feet help to hatch the eggs, holding them between the tops of the cormorant's feet and the warmth of its breast.

glossy back

white face

SUMMER PLUMAGE

white patch

♂ ♀

SIZE
Length 90 cm, Weight 2500 g

COLOUR
MALE Black plumage with bronze and blue overtones. White cheeks and chin. White thigh patches. Yellow bill.
FEMALE Same as male.
WINTER DIFFERENCES Duller; reduced white.

NEST
Twigs, seaweed and other available lining materials. On cliff ledges in colonies.

CALL
Deep croak.

RESIDENT/VISITOR
Resident.

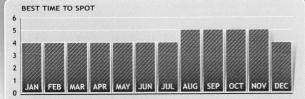

QUICK ID
- Long, hooked yellow bill
- White cheeks and chin
- Wide-spread wings when drying feathers
- Perched on buoys and in trees

BEST TIME TO SPOT

	JAN	FEB	MAR	APR	MAY	JUN	JUL	AUG	SEP	OCT	NOV	DEC

Did the bird have a yellow crown? ◯

Was it a very large, white bird with black wing tips? ◯

Were its legs short and black? ◯

Did it fly low over the water? ◯

Gannets have binocular vision, like humans, so they can judge a prey's distance accurately, and target it with startling accuracy.

My observations

my drawings and photos

Gannet
(Morus bassanus)

The gannet is one of the most spectacular diving birds in northern Atlantic waters. Plummeting from heights of up to 40 metres at speeds approaching 100 kilometres per hour, the gannet folds its wings as it approaches the sea, piercing the water like an arrow. It is helped by a lack of external nostrils, which could take up water from the impact. With a wingspan of almost 2 metres, it is one of our largest seabirds. It locates its prey from a great height, especially shoals of herring and mackerel, and fishermen have often been guided to good fishing areas by the sight of diving gannets.

SIZE
Length 91 cm, Weight 3000 g

COLOUR
MALE Mainly white, with yellowish head and nape. Black primary feathers on wings. Black around eyes.
FEMALE Same as male.
WINTER DIFFERENCES None.

NEST
Seaweed, earth and foliage, on rocky islands and coasts. Large colonies.

CALL
'Arrr' and 'kirra-kirra'.

RESIDENT/VISITOR
Resident breeder, spending non-breeding parts of year at sea, as far as the Azores, in the North Atlantic Ocean.

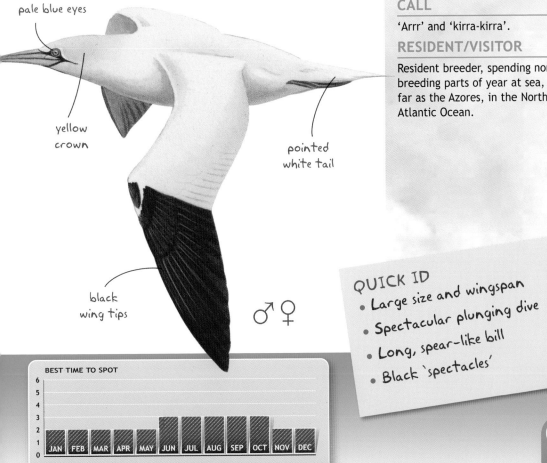

pale blue eyes

yellow crown

pointed white tail

black wing tips

♂♀

QUICK ID
- Large size and wingspan
- Spectacular plunging dive
- Long, spear-like bill
- Black 'spectacles'

BEST TIME TO SPOT

	JAN	FEB	MAR	APR	MAY	JUN	JUL	AUG	SEP	OCT	NOV	DEC
6												
5												
4												
3												
2												
1												
0												

Was it greenish-black all over? ◯

Did it look like a cormorant? ◯

If seen in summer,
did it have a crest? ◯

Were its legs grey and short? ◯

Juvenile shags still rely on adults for
food. They have dark brown plumage
and a white spot on the chin.

My observations

my drawings and photos

Shag
(Phalacrocorax aristotelis)

The shag is smaller and slimmer than its relative, the cormorant, with proportionally shorter wings and neck. It stays on wild, rocky coasts, not venturing inland. It is more at home in rough, deep waters than the cormorant, flying very close to the sea surface whatever the weather. It is a skilful and agile underwater swimmer, and feeds on shoal fish such as herrings and sand eels. The shag times its breeding so that the hatchlings appear at around the same time that sand eels are most plentiful.

SIZE
Length 76 cm, Weight 1850 g

COLOUR
MALE Dark metallic green plumage all over. Black bill. Yellowish gape.
FEMALE Same as male.
WINTER DIFFERENCES Loses the backward-pointing crest.

NEST
Seaweed, on a ledge on cliff, or in a cave.

CALL
'Karr' and 'arrk-arrk'.

RESIDENT/VISITOR
Resident.

crest

SUMMER PLUMAGE

black bill with yellow gape

metallic, greenish–black plumage

long, slender body

♂♀

QUICK ID
- Perches on rocks, not posts or buoys
- Upturned, bristly crest in spring
- Thinner bill than cormorant, and no facial white
- Dark green plumage

BEST TIME TO SPOT

	JAN	FEB	MAR	APR	MAY	JUN	JUL	AUG	SEP	OCT	NOV	DEC

Was it feeding head-down using a scything action? ◯

Was its bill long, curved and black? ◯

Did it have long, grey-blue legs? ◯

Was it in a rather noisy group? ◯

Avocets stoop forward as they feed. They prefer to wade through slightly salty water on fine-grained mud.

My observations

_____
_____
_____
_____
_____
_____
_____
_____
_____
_____
_____
_____

my drawings and photos

Avocet

(Recurvirostra avosetta)

The avocet uses its slender, upturned bill in the shallows to extract shrimps and other creatures from the mud. It sweeps its bill from side to side to dislodge them. It lives on a few estuaries in Britain, breeding on coastal lagoons in the east and south of the country. Absent from Britain for over a century due to drainage of habitats and hunting, this elegant wader returned in 1947 to East Anglia. It has successfully re-established itself due to careful management and conservation of its habitats by the Royal Society for the Protection of Birds and others.

SIZE
Length 43 cm, Weight 300–400 g

COLOUR
MALE Brilliant white, with contrasting black cap, back of neck, wing tips, wing patches, and upper body near base of wings. Legs long and greyish blue.
FEMALE Same as male.
WINTER DIFFERENCES None.

NEST
Hollow scraped in mud, some grass lining. In colonies.

CALL
'Pluit', 'plute' and alarm call, 'blik-blik-blik'.

RESIDENT/VISITOR
Some stay in winter. Others migrate to Asia and Africa.

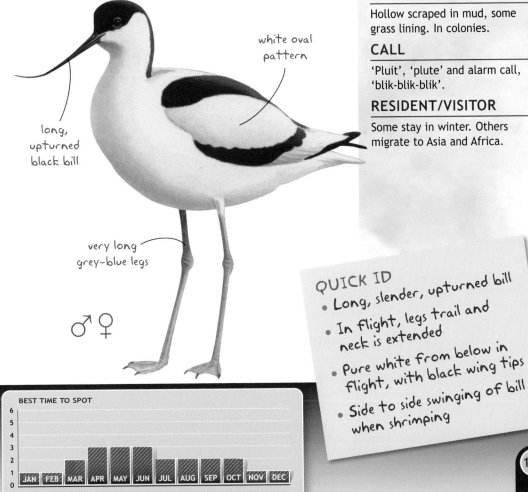

white oval pattern

long, upturned black bill

very long grey-blue legs

♂ ♀

QUICK ID
- Long, slender, upturned bill
- In flight, legs trail and neck is extended
- Pure white from below in flight, with black wing tips
- Side to side swinging of bill when shrimping

BEST TIME TO SPOT

	JAN	FEB	MAR	APR	MAY	JUN	JUL	AUG	SEP	OCT	NOV	DEC

Was its breast reddish-brown? ◯

Did it have a long, thin
upturned bill with a pink base? ◯

Was its back dappled
grey and chestnut? ◯

Were its wings grey? ◯

During the summer a male bar-tailed godwit has
a copper-red breast. This is its breeding plumage.

My observations

_____
_____
_____
_____
_____
_____
_____
_____
_____
_____
_____
_____
_____
_____
_____

my drawings and photos

Bar-tailed godwit

(Limosa lapponica)

Rarely seen inland, the bar-tailed godwit wades through the shallows on its long legs, probing the tidal mud and sandbanks of estuaries for food with its long bill. It is a sociable bird, which is usually seen in the company other waders, such as knots, redshanks, oystercatchers and curlews at the water's edge. The bar-tailed godwit feeds on worms, shellfish, crustaceans, water larvae and all sorts of insects. It is found in sandier areas than its relative, the black-tailed godwit, especially those rich in lugworms. When it sees the coiled worm cast appearing on the surface, it quickly plunges its beak deep into the sand before the lugworm can burrow out of reach.

SIZE

Length 41 cm, Weight 300 g

COLOUR

MALE Upperparts reddish brown, with black markings. Underparts rusty red, unmarked.
FEMALE Duller than male in summer.
WINTER DIFFERENCES Loses reddish tones. Underparts pale fawn.

NEST

Hollow on the ground, lined with grasses and dry leaves.

CALL

'Ved-ved-ved' in flight. Also 'kirruc-kirruc'.

RESIDENT/VISITOR

Winter visitor and passage migrant. Arrives on east coast between August and November. Leaves in the spring for Scandinavian and Siberian breeding grounds.

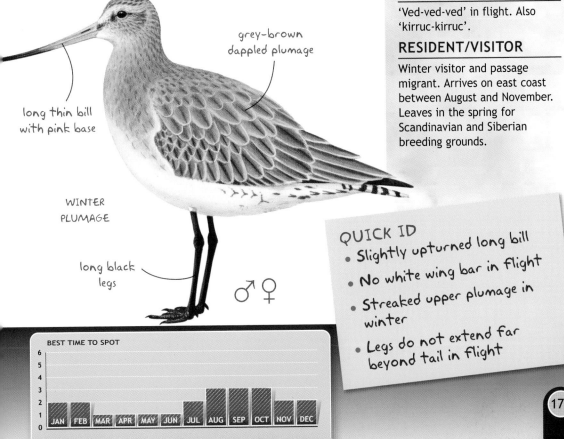

grey-brown dappled plumage

long thin bill with pink base

WINTER PLUMAGE

long black legs

♂ ♀

QUICK ID
- Slightly upturned long bill
- No white wing bar in flight
- Streaked upper plumage in winter
- Legs do not extend far beyond tail in flight

BEST TIME TO SPOT

	JAN	FEB	MAR	APR	MAY	JUN	JUL	AUG	SEP	OCT	NOV	DEC
6												
5												
4												
3												
2												
1												
0												

Was it a large bird? ◯

Was its overall colour
buff and brown streaks? ◯

Were its legs long and green? ◯

Did its long bill curve downwards? ◯

When a curlew flies it beats its wings
slowly and moves like a gull. Curlews often
fly in lines or in V-formations.

My observations

_____
_____
_____
_____
_____
_____
_____
_____
_____
_____
_____
_____
_____

my drawings and photos

Curlew
(Numenius arquata)

The curlew disperses in the spring from its winter flocks on estuaries and shores, and moves in pairs to nesting sites on moors, marshes and sand dunes. On the shore the curlew can often be seen with other waders, using its long, curved bill to excavate sand worms, crabs, shrimps and shellfish. Up on the moors in the breeding season, it feeds on insects and also eats plant material such as berries. The curlew is the largest of the European waders, and can sometimes be seen flying in formation with others with steady, gull-like wing beats. Its cry has an eerie, lonely quality, and can be heard at night as well as during the day.

SIZE
Length 50–60 cm,
Weight 700–1000 g

COLOUR
MALE Head, neck and front of body are streaky brown. Back darker. Lighter underparts. White rump.
FEMALE Similar colouring, longer bill.
WINTER DIFFERENCES None.

NEST
Grass-lined hollow in a field, marsh or moor.

CALL
'Curl-wee' and bubbling mating song.

RESIDENT/VISITOR
Some breed in Britain, migrating to Ireland in autumn. Others are passage migrants from Scandinavia in winter.

buff and brown colouring

long, downward-curved bill

dark green legs

♂ ♀

QUICK ID
- Very long, down-turned bill
- Distinctive call and mating song
- V-shaped white patch on back visible in flight
- Large size and long legs

BEST TIME TO SPOT

	JAN	FEB	MAR	APR	MAY	JUN	JUL	AUG	SEP	OCT	NOV	DEC

Did it have a longish, downward-curved bill? ◯

In winter was its overall appearance streaky black-and-white? ◯

Is a white wing bar visible in flight? ◯

Was it quite a dumpy little bird? ◯

In the summer, both male and female dunlins develop black underparts. Juveniles have mottled or streaked plumage.

My observations

_____
_____
_____
_____
_____
_____
_____
_____
_____
_____
_____
_____
_____
_____

my drawings and photos

Dunlin
(Calidris alpina)

The dunlin visits the British Isles in huge numbers for the winter, and is the UK's commonest wader. Dunlins run and quarrel as they probe beneath the surface of estuary mud and coastal sand for snails and ragworms. The large flocks fly in close formation, and will suddenly take off from the feeding site in unison, make a wheeling circuit, then land again to resume feeding. Birds that breed in Britain arrive in April, sometimes establishing nest sites at altitudes of up to 1000 metres in Scotland. At a distance, a close-packed flock of dunlins looks like moving smoke as they wheel and sweep over their feeding grounds.

SIZE
Length 16–19 cm, Weight 60 g

COLOUR
MALE Brown-black upperparts with red-and-brown markings. Pale underparts, back and neck. Black belly and legs.
FEMALE Reddish back of neck.
WINTER DIFFERENCES Grey-brown upperparts. White-and-grey underparts.

NEST
Compact grass bowl, hidden in vegetation on ground.

CALL
Harsh 'treer'.

RESIDENT/VISITOR
Some are winter visitors from Scandinavia and Siberia. Some breed in far northern Britain, migrating south in winter. Passage migrants from Iceland and Greenland pass through on their way south.

WINTER
PLUMAGE

grey crown

black-and-white tail

white belly

♂♀

QUICK ID
- Olive-black legs
- Fast-moving feeding flocks on ground
- Narrow white wing bar in flight
- Black belly in summer

BEST TIME TO SPOT

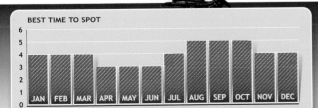

| JAN | FEB | MAR | APR | MAY | JUN | JUL | AUG | SEP | OCT | NOV | DEC |

Was it with other birds? ◯

Did it have long, black legs? ◯

Was its overall colour
grey and white in winter? ◯

Was it feeding on the tideline? ◯

My observations

Grey plovers often congregate in large
flocks, but they may squabble over the few
perches they can find at high tide.

my drawings and photos

Grey plover

(Pluvialis squatarola)

Increasing numbers of grey plovers are spending the winter in Britain. They breed in tundra areas of northern Russia and northern North America. In Britain the grey plover is found on coastal mudflats and shores, feeding on mussels and other shellfish as well as lugworms. It runs along the tideline in small groups, often mingling with other species, calling noisily as it forages for food.

SIZE

Length 27–30 cm,
Weight 200–250 g

COLOUR

MALE White-and-dark grey patterned cap and back. White forehead, side of neck, breast and rump. Black face, throat and underparts in summer.
FEMALE Same as male.
WINTER DIFFERENCES Pale throat and underparts, with grey-brown streaks. Dark grey and off-white upperparts.

NEST

Hollow in ground in Arctic tundra.

CALL

'Tlee-oo-ee'.

RESIDENT/VISITOR

Winter visitor and passage migrant.

WINTER PLUMAGE

grey-and-white plumage

short, thin black bill

long, black legs

♂♀

QUICK ID
- Black 'armpit' against white underwing in flight
- In summer, a black face and underparts framed in white
- White wing bar and rump visible in flight
- Heavy build and stout black bill

BEST TIME TO SPOT

	JAN	FEB	MAR	APR	MAY	JUN	JUL	AUG	SEP	OCT	NOV	DEC

Was it a small bird? ◯

Was its back brown? ◯

Did it have a black-and-white face and collar? ◯

Was its bill orange with a black tip? ◯

Ringed plover chicks hatch in the summer months, when there is an abundance of food. They have incomplete breast bands.

My observations

_____
_____
_____
_____
_____
_____
_____
_____
_____
_____
_____
_____
_____
_____

my drawings and photos

Ringed plover
(Charadrius hiaticula)

The ringed plover is short and stocky, and its black facial and breast markings contrast dramatically with its white front. Together with its brown cap and back, this means it is well camouflaged against the pebbles of the shingle beaches where it often nests. The ringed plover is a stop-start feeder, running along the water's edge and stopping to bob down and capture food items on the beach, including insects, worms and crustaceans. Like other shore birds it patters the mud with its feet to bring worms to the surface. It does not probe with its bill. Some ringed plovers breed inland, alongside rivers and lakes, and also in crop fields, moving back to the coast after breeding.

SIZE
Length 18–20 cm,
Weight 56–70 g

COLOUR
MALE Brown crown and back. White underparts. Black mask, brow band and collar. Yellow legs.
FEMALE Breast band and mask slightly browner than male.
WINTER DIFFERENCES White behind eye. Loses some neck and facial black.

NEST
Scraped hollow in sand, shingle or pebbles. On beaches and gravel pits.

CALL
'Too-li'.

RESIDENT/VISITOR
Both resident breeder and passage migrant.

brown crown

black face and eye mask

SUMMER PLUMAGE

white breast

yellow legs

♂

QUICK ID
• Distinctive black collar and mask
• Short yellow bill with black tip
• Prominent white upper wing bar in flight
• Running and bobbing feeding movements

BEST TIME TO SPOT

JAN	FEB	MAR	APR	MAY	JUN	JUL	AUG	SEP	OCT	NOV	DEC

Was it a large black-and-white bird? ◯

Did it have red eyes with an orange-red eye ring? ◯

Were its legs pink? ◯

Was its bill orange? ◯

In the summer, an oystercatcher may need to scour an estuary to find food for a brood of up to three hungry chicks.

My observations

_____
_____
_____
_____
_____
_____
_____
_____
_____
_____
_____
_____
_____

my drawings and photos

Oystercatcher
(Haematopus ostralegus)

The oystercatcher has a strong chisel shape at the end of its long, orange bill, which it uses to open tightly shut bivalves such as cockles and mussels. Everything about the oystercatcher is sturdy – bill, body and legs. It is usually seen in flocks along estuaries and seashores, where it works its way energetically along the edge of the water, feeding on shellfish and worms. Outside the breeding season, huge noisy flocks of mixed resident and migrant oystercatchers assemble on shore roosts. Occasionally oystercatchers are seen among gull flocks, following tractors on agricultural land for earthworms.

SIZE
Length 40–46 cm,
Weight 500–600 g

COLOUR
MALE Black head, upper breast and upperparts. White underparts. Orange-red eyes and bill. Pale pink legs.
FEMALE Same as male.
WINTER DIFFERENCES Duller, with white band across throat to sides of head.

NEST
Hollow scraped on the ground in sand, grass or pebbles. Dry riverbeds.

CALL
Loud 'kleep-kleep' and alarm call, 'gleea-gleea'.

RESIDENT/VISITOR
Resident breeding populations, swelled by many winter visitors from Iceland and Scandinavia.

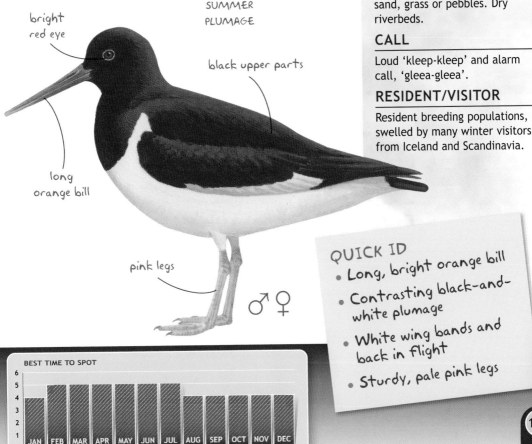

bright red eye

SUMMER PLUMAGE

black upper parts

long orange bill

pink legs

♂ ♀

QUICK ID
- Long, bright orange bill
- Contrasting black-and-white plumage
- White wing bands and back in flight
- Sturdy, pale pink legs

BEST TIME TO SPOT

6											
5											
4											
3											
2											
1											
0	JAN	FEB	MAR	APR	MAY	JUN	JUL	AUG	SEP	OCT	NOV	DEC

Was it a short-legged wading bird? ◯

Was the base of its bill yellow-orange in colour? ◯

Was its overall colouring black and grey? ◯

Were its legs yellow? ◯

Although purple sandpipers mostly eat small marine animals and insects, they also eat some plants, including seaweed.

My observations

_____
_____
_____
_____
_____
_____
_____
_____
_____
_____
_____
_____
_____
_____
_____

my drawings and photos

Purple sandpiper
(Calidris maritima)

A small number of purple sandpipers breed in Scotland, but it is mainly a visitor to the British Isles between autumn and spring, and appears on most coasts. It is usually very tame in the presence of humans. Outside the breeding season its favourite feeding territory is the wave-splash area along rocky coasts. It forages busily in small flocks through the seaweed-covered boulders for winkles, small crabs and other titbits, which it picks out with its shortish, slightly curving bill. Its dark winter plumage provides it with an excellent camouflage against a background of wet rocks and exposed beds of weed.

SIZE
Length 20–22 cm,
Weight 55–80 g

COLOUR
MALE Dark, slate-brown upperparts, head and breast. White belly. Spotted flanks.
FEMALE Same as male.
SUMMER DIFFERENCES Paler, more spotted upperparts. Reddish back. Legs and base of bill more orange.

NEST
Untidy, straw, grass, feathers. Usually in a hole in trees, buildings, cliffs, nest-boxes.

CALL
'Wit', and 'weet-wit'.

RESIDENT/VISITOR
Winter visitor from Greenland and Scandinavia. A few pairs are resident breeders in Scotland.

WINTER PLUMAGE

grey-brown plumage

yellow-orange base to bill

♂♀

yellow legs

QUICK ID
- Short yellow legs
- Yellow-orange base to bill
- Stocky, plump body
- Forages amongst rocks and seaweed

BEST TIME TO SPOT

	JAN	FEB	MAR	APR	MAY	JUN	JUL	AUG	SEP	OCT	NOV	DEC

Was it with other birds? ◯

Were its legs long and red? ◯

Was its tail short, square and black and white? ◯

Did it have a red base to its bill? ◯

This redshank is in its summer plumage, with a white belly covered in black spots. It makes loud ringing calls from its perch.

My observations

_____
_____
_____
_____
_____
_____
_____
_____
_____
_____
_____
_____

my drawings and photos

Redshank
(Tringa totanus)

The redshank breeds throughout the British Isles, nesting in marshes, moorlands and meadows. Outside the breeding season it moves to coastal flatlands and estuaries. Here it swims and wades as it probes the mud for molluscs, worms, crustaceans and insects. The redshank is a noisy bird, emitting loud alarm calls when intruders approach its nest. It does this both from perches, such as fence posts, and while flying. The male has a spectacular courting dance, approaching the female with wings raised to display the white under-surfaces, and performing a slow, high-stepping walk with his long red legs. He then begins to flutter his wings, leaving the ground entirely with each step, trilling noisily.

SIZE
Length 28 cm, Weight 130 g

COLOUR
MALE Greyish brown back with dark streaks. Whitish underparts with brown markings. White trailing edge to wing. White rump. Red legs.
FEMALE Same as male.
WINTER DIFFERENCES Greyer upperparts. Whiter underparts, less spotted.

NEST
Cup-shaped, made of grass, on the ground in marsh or similar. Concealed by vegetation.

CALL
'Tu-yu-yu'.

RESIDENT/VISITOR
Resident breeders, plus passage migrants that visit in winter from Iceland and northern Europe.

WINTER
PLUMAGE

♂ ♀

red legs

dark brown bill with red base

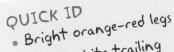

QUICK ID
- Bright orange-red legs
- Broad white trailing edge to wing
- Red base to bill, black tip
- Stands on raised perches such as posts

BEST TIME TO SPOT

JAN	FEB	MAR	APR	MAY	JUN	JUL	AUG	SEP	OCT	NOV	DEC

Was it a medium-sized bird? ◯

Did it have dark green legs? ◯

Was it with a lot of similar birds? ◯

Did it have an eye stripe? ◯

Large flocks of knots gather by the sea, waiting for the tide to recede. As the water moves back, the birds move in to find food.

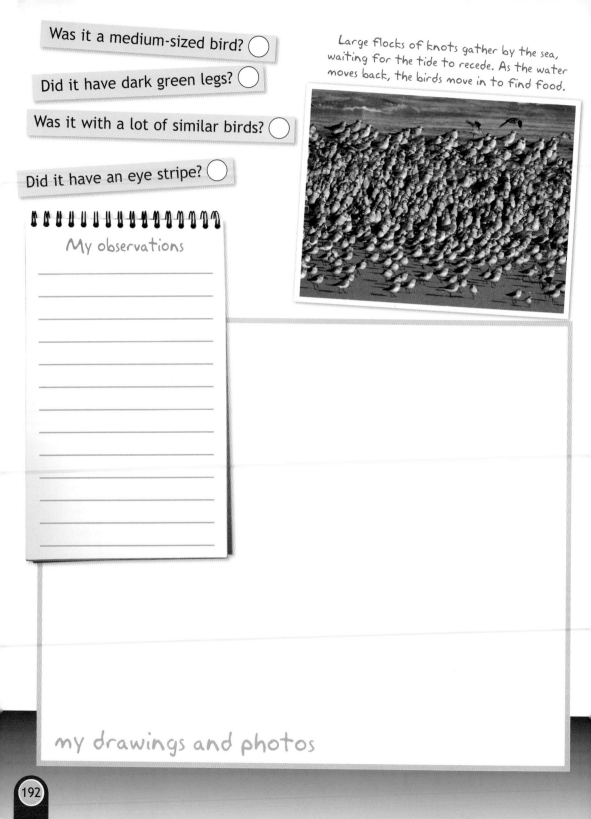

My observations

my drawings and photos

Knot
(Calidris canuta)

The knot is a sociable little wader. It is usually seen in large flocks on mudflats and sandy estuaries in winter in Britain, mainly on east and northwest coasts. It breeds in the Arctic regions of Europe, North America and Asia. The close-packed flocks cover the feeding ground like a moving carpet, all probing rapidly for food. Occasionally they take to the air to perform complicated formation aerobatics, all turning and wheeling at exactly the same time. A flock may contain many thousands of birds. They feed on small shellfish such as cockles and immature mussels.

SIZE
Length 25 cm, Weight 150 g

COLOUR
MALE Pale grey-brown upperparts. Paler underparts, flecked with darker markings.
FEMALE Same as male.
WINTER DIFFERENCES Distinctive brick-red head and underparts. Black-brown markings on russet upperparts.

NEST
Scraped hollow in tundra lined with lichens.

CALL
'Nutt' and whistling 'twit-twit'.

RESIDENT/VISITOR
Winter visitor from Arctic.

eye stripe

grey back

short, straight bill

WINTER PLUMAGE

dark green legs

♂ ♀

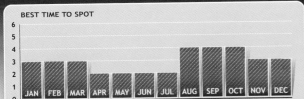

BEST TIME TO SPOT

| JAN | FEB | MAR | APR | MAY | JUN | JUL | AUG | SEP | OCT | NOV | DEC |

Was it feeding in a small flock? ◯

Was it quite a small bird? ◯

Did it have a black bill and legs? ◯

Was it black at the bend of its wing? ◯

Sanderlings are whiter than other members of the sandpiper family. They move quickly through the water, grabbing food.

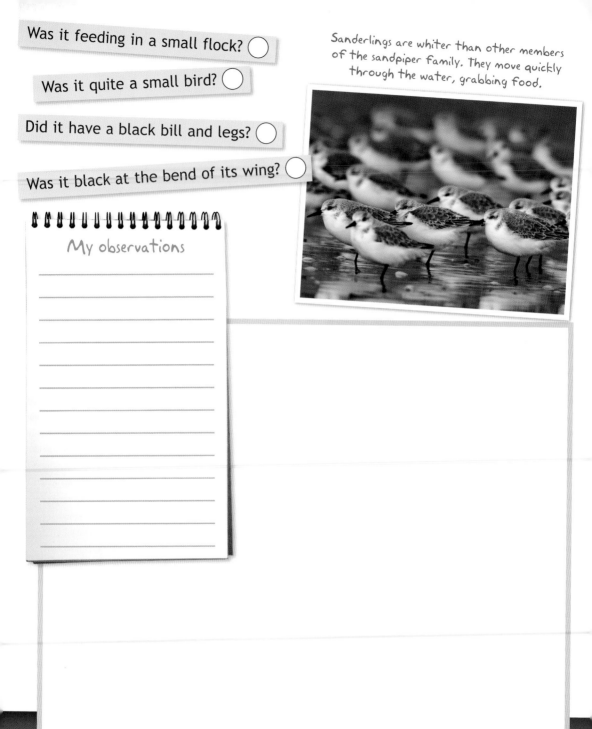

My observations

_____
_____
_____
_____
_____
_____
_____
_____
_____
_____
_____
_____

my drawings and photos

Sanderling
(Calidris alba)

The sanderling is always on the move, usually running. On the ground the flocks run like streams of insects as the birds hurry and bustle in their continual quest for worms, shellfish and shrimps. In the air flocks fly in co-ordinated movement over mudflats. The sanderling breeds in the high Arctic regions of Canada, Greenland, Scandinavia and Siberia. It migrates in winter as far south as Australasia, though some winter much further north, including those which are seen in Britain. The sanderling likes to feed right at the edge of the water where the waves break, scurrying towards the retreating water to pick up morsels, then running back up the beach as the waves return.

SIZE
Length 20–21 cm,
Weight 50–60 g

COLOUR
MALE Pale grey back with faint dark markings. Dark shoulder patch. Pure white underparts. Black legs.
FEMALE Same as male.
SUMMER DIFFERENCES Light chestnut head, neck and breast. Back chestnut mottled with black.

NEST
Shallow hole scraped in Arctic tundra.

CALL
'Tvik-tvik'.

RESIDENT/VISITOR
Winter visitor all round the coast. Passage migrant to and from Arctic. Some non-breeders stay all summer.

short, straight black bill

WINTER PLUMAGE

black-and-white tail

white breast

black legs

♂ ♀

QUICK ID
- Large white wing bar in flight
- Black bill and legs
- Runs close to waves when feeding
- Spotless white belly

BEST TIME TO SPOT

| JAN | FEB | MAR | APR | MAY | JUN | JUL | AUG | SEP | OCT | NOV | DEC |

Was it stocky with short, orange legs? ◯

Was its bill thin, short and black? ◯

Were its head markings complex? ◯

Was it turning stones or seaweed for food? ◯

The breeding plumage of a turnstone is stunning, with bold black-and-white patterns and chestnut wing feathers.

My observations

my drawings and photos

Turnstone

(Arenaria interpres)

The turnstones wintering in Britain have bred in Canada and Greenland. The passage migrants passing through Britain in spring and autumn breed in Scandinavia and winter in Africa. The turnstone has earned its name from the way it overturns stones, moves seaweed and digs sand to catch the tiny creatures that scatter as they are exposed. Rocky coasts provide it with abundant supplies of winkles, mussels and limpets, as well as the fast-moving invertebrates flushed out from beneath stones and seaweed patches. Sometimes several turnstones co-operate to overturn a heavy stone that one bird cannot manage alone.

SIZE

Length 21–25 cm,
Weight 80–150 g

COLOUR

MALE Dull brown upperparts. White underparts. Dark grey bib.
FEMALE Duller than male.
WINTER DIFFERENCES
Chestnut-and-black upperparts. Black bands on white face and neck.

NEST

On ground on rocky terrain and coastal islands.

CALL

'Tuk-a-tuk' and 'kyug'.

RESIDENT/VISITOR

Winter visitor, and spring/autumn passage migrant.

chestnut-and-black colouring

white throat

WINTER PLUMAGE

orange legs

QUICK ID
• Stone-turning activity
• Short-billed and stocky
• Black-and-white wing
• White undersides and dark 'bib'

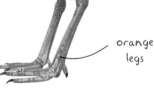

BEST TIME TO SPOT

| JAN | FEB | MAR | APR | MAY | JUN | JUL | AUG | SEP | OCT | NOV | DEC |

Did it have a black tail with grey outer feathers? ◯

Was it streaky grey and brown in colour? ◯

Did it have a faint eyebrow? ◯

Was its call harsh but clear? ◯

My observations

_____
_____
_____
_____
_____
_____
_____
_____
_____
_____
_____
_____
_____

In the summer, rock pipits move closer to cliff edges and rocky islands to feed and forage among grass and other plants.

my drawings and photos

Rock pipit

(Anthus petrosus)

Rock pipits are hard to see as they forage among coastal rocks and seaweed, feeding on tiny molluscs. Their dark colouring is a good camouflage among the rocks and vegetation, and they are often only noticed when they take to their wings, flitting erratically between rocks and along the shore. The rock pipit's calls and song are particularly loud, as it has to compete with the general noise of waves crashing on a rocky shore. In winter it may extend its food searches to estuaries and mudflats, and sometimes appears at inland reservoirs. Rock pipits are found around most of the coastline except for stretches without rocky shores.

SIZE
Length 16 cm, Weight 21–30 g

COLOUR
MALE Dark greyish brown upperparts. Buff underparts. Speckled throat and breast. Pale line through eye. Dark legs. Grey outer tail feathers.
FEMALE Same as male.
WINTER DIFFERENCES Streaks disappear leaving undersides dark.

NEST
Grass, hair, seaweed, in rocky crevice, or concealed in shore vegetation.

CALL
'Peep-peep' alarm call. Males deliver a trill song in flight.

RESIDENT/VISITOR
Resident breeders, with some Scandinavian migrants.

streaky patterning

black tail with grey outer feathers

SUMMER PLUMAGE

dark legs

♂ ♀

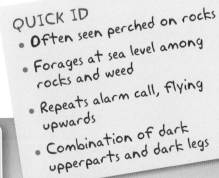

QUICK ID
- Often seen perched on rocks
- Forages at sea level among rocks and weed
- Repeats alarm call, flying upwards
- Combination of dark upperparts and dark legs

BEST TIME TO SPOT

JAN	FEB	MAR	APR	MAY	JUN	JUL	AUG	SEP	OCT	NOV	DEC

Was the bird with others? ◯

Did it have a black-and-white tail? ◯

Was its bill black and stubby? ◯

Was a lot of the bird white? ◯

Snow buntings breed in the Arctic, where snow still lies on the ground, so a white plumage camouflages them at this vulnerable time.

My observations

my drawings and photos

Snow bunting

(Plectrophenax nivalis)

The snow bunting is a bird of rocks, from the rocky tops of northern mountains, to the rocky shores of Scotland and eastern England. In winter it appears along North Sea coasts in flocks. Snow buntings call noisily as they feed on seeds and insects. The flock moves across the ground in a series of running, pecking and fluttering movements. Because of the large amount of white in their plumage, snow buntings are sometimes known locally as snowflakes. A small number of snow buntings may now be regular breeders in the Cairngorm mountains and other Scottish ranges, but most are winter visitors.

SIZE

Length 16.5 cm, Weight 30–40 g

COLOUR

MALE Rusty buff head and throat band. Brown back with dark streaks. Underparts creamy, white wing patches.
FEMALE Wing patches smaller than in male.
SUMMER DIFFERENCES Male has a white head and body, contrasting black on wings. Female has grey upperparts, off-white underparts.

NEST

Grass, moss, feathers, in rocky crevice.

CALL

'Brrr' and 'tsrrr'. Trilling song.

RESIDENT/VISITOR

Winter visitor, rarely breeding in Scottish mountains.

colourful cap

WINTER PLUMAGE

stubby bill

white undersides

white on wing

♂ ♀

QUICK ID
- Bouncy, wave-like flight
- White in wings and tail visible in flight
- Breeding male stark black-and-white contrasts
- Rusty head colouring in winter

BEST TIME TO SPOT

6												
5												
4												
3												
2												
1												
0	JAN	FEB	MAR	APR	MAY	JUN	JUL	AUG	SEP	OCT	NOV	DEC

Was its plumage black? ◯

Were its legs grey? ◯

Did it have a yellow bill? ◯

Was it with other ducks? ◯

In March, large numbers of common scoters leave British shores to breed elsewhere. They return around October.

My observations

_____
_____
_____
_____
_____
_____
_____
_____
_____
_____
_____
_____
_____

my drawings and photos

Common scoter

(Melanitta nigra)

The male common scoter is the only duck with totally black plumage. Common scoters breed on lakes and pools in the Arctic tundra, and move to coasts in winter. They feed by diving for molluscs, especially mussels. A few pairs breed on lochs in Scotland, but most common scoters that appear in British waters are winter visitors seen swimming and feeding off the coast. They are often in the company of velvet scoters. The common scoter spends most of its time at sea, and is capable of diving to great depths, and stays underwater for up to a minute at a time. It is now on the IUCN's red list of threatened species.

SIZE
Length 45–55 cm,
Weight 700–1400 g

COLOUR
MALE Black plumage. Yellow on upper bill.
FEMALE Chocolate brown. Paler cheeks and neck. Black bill.
WINTER DIFFERENCES None.

NEST
Concealed on ground, near water.

CALL
Male – low, piping call.
Female – grating call.

RESIDENT/VISITOR
Winter visitor from Arctic. A few resident breeders in Scotland.

yellow bill with
black knob at base

black
plumage

RARE

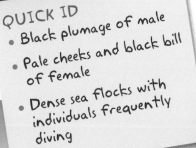

QUICK ID
• Black plumage of male
• Pale cheeks and black bill of female
• Dense sea flocks with individuals frequently diving

BEST TIME TO SPOT

6											
5											
4											
3											
2											
1											
0	JAN	FEB	MAR	APR	MAY	JUN	JUL	AUG	SEP	OCT	NOV	DEC

Did it have a flat forehead? ◯

Was its breast tinged with pink? ◯

Were its legs short and brown? ◯

Was its back white? ◯

Female eiders incubate their eggs in ground nests. Once the chicks have hatched, they are often kept in crèches to protect them from predators.

My observations

_____
_____
_____
_____
_____
_____
_____
_____
_____
_____
_____
_____
_____

my drawings and photos

Eider

(Somateria mollissima)

Famous for the heat-retaining qualities of its down feathers, the eider duck is most commonly seen in the British Isles in Scottish coastal waters. It is a resident breeder, with increasing numbers of breeding pairs in both Scotland and Ireland. Eiders dive for molluscs, often at low tide, when inshore waters are shallower. From time to time they come out of the water to rest on rocks and islets. The female eider sometimes goes without food for two or three weeks while incubating the eggs. After hatching, the ducklings are often looked after by one or more females, who oversee several broods.

SIZE

Length 50–71 cm,
Weight 1500–2800 g

COLOUR

MALE Black crown. White head, neck and breast. Green markings on back of head and upper bill. Rosy flush on breast. Black underparts.
FEMALE Reddish brown upperparts. Pale brown underparts, barred with dark grey.
WINTER DIFFERENCES None.

NEST

Grass, seaweed, down. On ground in the open, or in a rocky crevice.

CALL

Male 'uhuu-uhuu'. Female 'korr-korr'.

RESIDENT/VISITOR

Resident breeder and winter visitor.

black crown

white back

pink tinge to breast

♂

short brown legs

QUICK ID
- White breast and back, black underparts (male)
- Feathers coming down to peak over bill
- Green markings on head (male)
- Wedge-shaped bill and head

BEST TIME TO SPOT

6												
5												
4												
3												
2												
1												
0	JAN	FEB	MAR	APR	MAY	JUN	JUL	AUG	SEP	OCT	NOV	DEC

Was its tail long and pointed? ◯

Did it have bold black-
and-white markings? ◯

Did it have short, black legs? ◯

Was its head large? ◯

My observations

_____
_____
_____
_____
_____
_____
_____
_____
_____
_____
_____
_____
_____

Long-tailed ducks fly with fast wing beats
and often skim close to the water's surface
before splashing down heavily.

my drawings and photos

Long-tailed duck

(Clangula hyemalis)

The long-tailed duck is a winter visitor. It is seen most commonly between northeast England and the Shetland Islands, and in the Outer Hebrides. A large proportion – up to 75 per cent – of the British winter population lives around the waters and inlets of the Moray Firth. The long-tailed duck breeds in northern tundra lands, moving south to winter on the sea. It dives for its food of molluscs and crustaceans, and prefers to spend its winter break in shallow waters. It is a fast flier, and has no fear of harsh weather conditions, swimming and diving however rough the sea.

SIZE

Length 40–53 cm,
Weight 600–800 g

COLOUR

MALE White all over, with dark cheek patch. Black markings on back and wings. Long black tail. Pink band across black bill.
FEMALE Duller and browner than male. No long tail. Grey ear patch.
SUMMER DIFFERENCES Male – dark brown upperparts.

NEST

On ground in tundra on lake islands.

CALL

'Calloo'.

RESIDENT/VISITOR

Winter visitor.

pink bill

WINTER PLUMAGE

long pointed tail

black-and-white markings

♂

QUICK ID
- Unique long tail of male
- Dark wings above and below visible in flight
- Dark bill with pink band (male)
- Dark circular cheek patch (male)

BEST TIME TO SPOT

6
5
4
3
2
1
0

JAN | FEB | MAR | APR | MAY | JUN | JUL | AUG | SEP | OCT | NOV | DEC

Was the duck a slim shape? ◯

Did it have a dark green
head with a double crest? ◯

Were its legs and bill red? ◯

Was its tail short and grey? ◯

Female red-breasted mergansers have crests
like the males, but they are less impressive.
Females like to nest near grassy banks.

My observations

_____
_____
_____
_____
_____
_____
_____
_____
_____
_____
_____

my drawings and photos

Red-breasted merganser

(Mergus serrator)

The red-breasted merganser is a bird of inlets, shallow coastal waters, inland lakes and rivers. It is a resident breeder in Ireland and Scotland, with some pairs in northwest England and Wales. It is a saw-billed duck, so named because it has a serrated edge to its beak, which helps it keep a grip on fish caught underwater. It flies low and fast over the water's surface, and is often to be seen swimming along with its head submerged as it scans for fish. After diving and catching a fish, the red-breasted merganser brings it to the surface to swallow it, then performs a wing-flapping display, followed by a drink of seawater.

SIZE

Length 52–58 cm,
Weight 900–1200 g

COLOUR

MALE Green-black head with crest. Spotted chestnut breast. Grey flanks. White underparts and collar. Red bill.
FEMALE Grey body. Chestnut head and crest merging into neck. White wing patches.
WINTER DIFFERENCES Male plumage is duller. Rusty brown head and chest.

NEST

Grass, leaves and down, on the ground. Hidden among plants and boulders.

CALL

Male 'yiuv' and 'orr'. Female 'rok-rok-rok'.

RESIDENT/VISITOR

Resident breeder. Some Scandinavian winter visitors.

red bill

dark green head

double crest

SUMMER PLUMAGE

speckled breast

♂

QUICK ID
- Green-black head of male in summer
- Double crest at the back of head
- Red bill and legs
- Slender build

BEST TIME TO SPOT

6											
5											
4											
3											
2											
1											
0											
JAN	FEB	MAR	APR	MAY	JUN	JUL	AUG	SEP	OCT	NOV	DEC

Was it a large bird? ◯

Did it have a rusty-coloured band on its breast? ◯

Were its head and neck dark green? ◯

Were its legs pink? ◯

Shelducks are territorial birds, and males can be aggressive, fighting one another over territory and mates.

My observations

_____
_____
_____
_____
_____
_____
_____
_____
_____
_____
_____
_____

my drawings and photos

Shelduck

(Tadorna tadorna)

The colourful shelduck pairs up with its mate for more than one season. Each pair establishes separate nesting and feeding territories, often a considerable distance apart, and the female chooses a burrow in which to lay her eggs. When the young are hatched the parents escort them on what can be a long walk to the water where they can feed. They travel in single file, with one parent leading, and the other bringing up the rear. The shelduck is the largest duck in the British Isles, feeding mainly on muddy estuaries and sandy shores. Its broad bill acts as a sieve for separating molluscs from mud.

SIZE

Length 60–70 cm,
Weight 800–1400 g

COLOUR

MALE Brilliant white body and wings. Green-black head, neck, base of wings and rear underside. Wide rust band around body and breast. Green and rust patches to rear of wings. Black wing tips. Coral-red bill with knob.

FEMALE Duller than male. White facial marks. No knob on bill.

WINTER DIFFERENCES Duller.

NEST

Down-lined, in a burrow or hole in tree.

CALL

Male, low whistle, 'huee'. Female, deep rapid quacks, 'ak-ak-ak'.

RESIDENT/VISITOR

Resident breeder.

dark green head

rusty-coloured band on chest

reddish-pink bill with knob

♂

QUICK ID
• Reddish-pink bill of male with knob at base
• Goose-like shape and size
• Vivid black, white and rust contrasting colours
• White, black, green and rust wings in flight

BEST TIME TO SPOT

	JAN	FEB	MAR	APR	MAY	JUN	JUL	AUG	SEP	OCT	NOV	DEC

Did it have a dark head and white neck flash? ◯

Was its rump white? ◯

Did it have a black throat? ◯

Was its crown black? ◯

Outside of the breeding season, brent geese eat a diet mostly of seaweeds and eelgrass. At breeding time, they eat land plants.

My observations

my drawings and photos

Brent goose

(Branta bernicla)

The brent goose eats plant food for the most part, feeding on eel grass, algae and marsh plants in the salt marshes and muddy estuaries where it grazes. It also eats young cereal plants, and picks up the fallen grain from stubble after harvesting. Like most geese it prefers company, and feeds, flies and roosts in close-packed flocks. There are two branches of the brent goose family. The dark-bellied birds fly to southern British estuaries from Russia. The pale-bellied birds fly from Greenland to Ireland, and from Spitzbergen to northeast England. The brent goose is the smallest of the European geese.

SIZE

Length 55–60 cm,
Weight 1200–1500 g

COLOUR

MALE Black head, neck and chest. Dark barred belly (southern coasts). Pale barred belly (northeast and Ireland). White rump and narrow collar.
FEMALE Same as male.
WINTER DIFFERENCES None.

NEST

Rocky hollow lined with down.

CALL

'Rronk-rronk'.

RESIDENT/VISITOR

Winter visitor from Arctic.

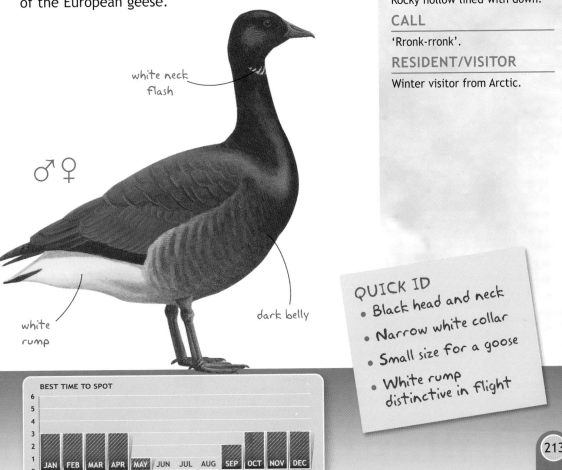

white neck flash

♂♀

white rump

dark belly

QUICK ID
- Black head and neck
- Narrow white collar
- Small size for a goose
- White rump distinctive in flight

BEST TIME TO SPOT

6												
5												
4												
3												
2												
1												
0	JAN	FEB	MAR	APR	MAY	JUN	JUL	AUG	SEP	OCT	NOV	DEC

Checklist

A checklist of birds that can be seen in the British Isles.
Tick each bird you see and add the date you saw it.

STARLINGS AND THRUSHES   DATE

- [ ] Starling ....
- [ ] Song thrush ....
- [ ] Mistle thrush..
- [ ] Redwing ....
- [ ] Fieldfare..
- [ ] Blackbird ....
- [ ] Nightingale..

TITS   DATE

- [ ] Blue tit ....
- [ ] Coal tit ....
- [ ] Great tit ....
- [ ] Long-tailed tit ....
- [ ] Marsh tit ....
- [ ] Goldcrest..
- [ ] Treecreeper..

FINCHES

DATE

- [ ] Brambling ....
- [ ] Bullfinch ....
- [ ] Chaffinch ....
- [ ] Goldfinch ....
- [ ] Greenfinch ....
- [ ] Siskin ....

SPARROWS AND BUNTINGS

DATE

- [ ] House sparrow ....
- [ ] Reed bunting ....
- [ ] Dunnock ....

WOODPECKERS

DATE

- [ ] Green woodpecker ....
- [ ] Great spotted woodpecker ....
- [ ] Lesser spotted woodpecker ....

KINGFISHERS

DATE

☐ Kingfisher...

OWLS

DATE

☐ Barn owl..

☐ Tawny owl...

WARBLERS

DATE

☐ Garden warbler ....

☐ Willow warbler ....

☐ Chiffchaff ....

☐ Blackcap..

SWIFTS, SWALLOWS AND MARTINS

DATE

☐ Swift ....

☐ Swallow..

☐ House martin ....

Checklist

WAGTAILS, FLYCATCHERS AND CHATS
DATE

☐ Pied wagtail ....
☐ Spotted flycatcher...
☐ Robin..
☐ Wren ....

PIGEONS AND DOVES
DATE

☐ Woodpigeon..
☐ Cuckoo..
☐ Stock dove ....
☐ Collared dove...

BIRDS OF PREY
DATE

☐ Peregrine falcon ....
☐ Sparrowhawk ....

CROWS

DATE

- ☐ Carrion crow ....
- ☐ Jackdaw ....
- ☐ Magpie ....
- ☐ Jay ....
- ☐ Rook ....

HERONS

DATE

- ☐ Grey heron ....

GAME BIRDS

DATE

- ☐ Pheasant ....

WILDFOWL

DATE

- ☐ Mallard ....
- ☐ Mute swan ....

PARROTS

DATE

- ☐ Ring-necked parakeet ....

Checklist

GULLS, TERNS AND SKUAS DATE

- [ ] Arctic tern ....
- [ ] Common tern ....
- [ ] Little tern ....
- [ ] Sandwich tern ....
- [ ] Black-headed gull..
- [ ] Common gull ....
- [ ] Great black-backed gull ....
- [ ] Herring gull ....
- [ ] Lesser black-backed gull ....
- [ ] Mediterranean gull ....
- [ ] Arctic skua..
- [ ] Great skua ....

CHOUGHS DATE

- [ ] Chough...

DOVES

DATE

☐ Rock dove ....

AUKS AND FULMARS

DATE

☐ Guillemot...
☐ Black guillemot..
☐ Fulmar ....
☐ Kittiwake ....
☐ Puffin ....
☐ Razorbill ....
☐ Manx shearwater ....

GANNETS AND CORMORANTS

DATE

☐ Cormorant..
☐ Gannet..
☐ Shag ....

Checklist

WADERS   DATE

- [ ] Avocet...
- [ ] Bar-tailed godwit ....
- [ ] Curlew ....
- [ ] Dunlin..
- [ ] Grey plover ....
- [ ] Ringed plover..
- [ ] Oystercatcher ....
- [ ] Purple sandpiper..
- [ ] Redshank ....
- [ ] Knot ....
- [ ] Sanderling..
- [ ] Turnstone...

PIPITS AND BUNTINGS   DATE

- [ ] Rock pipit ....
- [ ] Snow bunting ....

DUCKS AND GEESE   DATE

- [ ] Common scoter..
- [ ] Eider ....
- [ ] Long-tailed duck ....
- [ ] Red-breasted merganser...
- [ ] Shelduck..
- [ ] Brent goose ....

Index

First published in 2006 by
Miles Kelly Publishing Ltd
Harding's Barn, Bardfield End Green,
Thaxted, Essex, CM6 3PX, UK

Copyright © 2006 Miles Kelly Publishing Ltd

This edition updated 2014 and printed 2015

4 6 8 10 9 7 5 3

Publishing Director Belinda Gallagher
Creative Director Jo Cowan
Designers Simon Lee, Venita Kidwai
Cover Designer Jo Cowan
Production Elizabeth Collins,
Caroline Kelly
Reprographics Stephan Davis,
Thom Allaway
Consultant Camilla de la Bedoyere
Assets Lorraine King

ISBN 978-1-78209-126-4

Printed in China

British Library Cataloguing-in-Publication
Data
A catalogue record for this book is
available from the British Library

Made with paper from a sustainable forest

www.mileskelly.net
info@mileskelly.net

acknowledgements

The publishers would like to thank the following artists who have
contributed to this book:
Alan Harris, Ian Jackson, Stuart Jackson-Carter

All other artworks from the Miles Kelly Artwork Bank

The publishers would like to thank the following sources for the use
of their photographs:
Cover Geanina Bechea/Shutterstock.com

FLPA 56 Neil Bowman; 78 David Hosking; 86 Juan-Carlos Munoz/
Biosphoto; 94 Mike Jones; 102 Roger Tidman; 104 Steve Trewhella;
144 Roger Wilmshurst; 148 Andrew Parkinson; 150 Steve Young;
152 Roger Wilmshurst; 156 Gianpiero Ferrari; 182 Paul Sawer;
192 Frits Van Daalen/FN/Minden; 198 Roger Wilmshurst; 208 David
Tipling

Fotolia.com 7tl Sharpshot #1123381; 44 Tomasz Kubis; 46 eric
weight; 88 Christian Marx; 106 Kerioak;

iStockphoto.com 22 Andrew Howe; 30 Charlie Bishop;
68 stevephotos; 174 Andrew Howe

Photoshot 206 David Tipling

rspb-images.com 58 David Kjaer; 90 Mark Hamblin; 96 Ernie Janes;
164 Mike Read; 202 Mark Hamblin

Shutterstock.com 6bl rng; 6tr Morgan Lane Photography; 7tr Kletr;
7br Ivan M Munoz; 8tr mrHanson; 8tl aggressor; 8b Tony Brindley;
9t chronicler; 9bl Tropinina Olga; 9br prudkov; 10 Menno Schaefer;
12 Grant Glendinning; 14 Vishnevskiy Vasily; 16 BogdanBoev;
18 Sandy Maya Matzen; 20 IbajaUsap; 24 Anders Nyberg; 26 Kletr;
28 Roman Slavik; 32 Gertjan Hooijer; 34 Martin Fowler; 36 iliuta
goean; 38 Maksimilian; 40 Alexei Novikov; 42 Vitaly Ilyasov;
48 Miroslav Hlavko; 50 Arto Hakola; 52 Vishnevskiy Vasily;
54 Vishnevskiy Vasily; 60 Grant Glendinning; 62 Vishnevskiy Vasily;
64 Marek CECH; 66 bikeriderlondon; 70 Vishnevskiy Vasily; 72 Vitaly
Ilyasov; 74 xpixel; 76 Cristian Mihai; 82 RazvanZinica; 84 Mircea
Bezergheanu; 92 Zacarias Pereira da Mata; 98 PetrP; 100 Sue
Robinson; 108 Mircea Bezergheanu; 110 IbajaUsap; 112 xpixel;
114 Zacarias Pereira da Mata; 116 Peter Wollinga; 118 Stargazer;
120 Steve Byland; 122 Chrislofoto; 126 Wild Arctic Pictures;
128 Sergey Uryadnikov; 130 Jeff Lim C.W.; 132 Norman Bateman;
134 Chrislofotos; 138 Elliotte Rusty Harold; 140 trubach;
142 trubach; 146 toomasili; 154 Ewan Chesser; 158 TTphoto;
160 Gail Johnson; 162 Atlaspix; 166 krisgillam; 168 A.von Dueren;
170 Gail Johnson; 172 Tony Brindley; 176 Anders Nyberg; 178 Mark
Medcalf; 180 nawrocki; 184 ArvydasS; 186 David Dohnal; 188 Elliotte
Rusty Harold; 190 Arto Hakola; 194 Menno Schaefer; 196 Stubblefield
Photography; 200 Francis Bossé; 204 Daniel Prudek; 210 Mircea
Bezergheanu; 212 AndreAnita

All other photographs from: digitalSTOCK, digitalvision,
Dreamstime.com, Fotolia.com, iStockphoto.com, John Foxx,
PhotoAlto, PhotoDisc, PhotoEssentials, PhotoPro, Stockbyte, WTPL